To Wendy
Much Love and enjoy
mother Hood

IN THE MOMENT

Love

Mick E.

IN THE MOMENT

MICK E. JONES

Library of Congress Control Number: 2013909266
ISBN: Hardcover   978-1-4836-4433-2
                 Softcover   978-1-4836-4432-5
                 Ebook   978-1-4836-4434-9

This book was printed in the United States of America.

Rev. date: 09/25/2013

To order additional copies of this book, contact:
Xlibris LLC
1-888-795-4274
www.Xlibris.com
Orders@Xlibris.com
125304

CONTENTS

WHY DO I WANT TO BE PUBLISHED?

That is the question I have been asked to answer. Questions can be probed, rephrased, mulled over, or set aside. Answers, however, need to be experienced. Why do I want to be published? As my answer unfolds, remember, the question is rigid, but the answer is organic. It is a *living explanation* that will make plain, or at least understandable, the logical justification and marketability of *In the Moment*. At present, it is an unpublished manuscript. I have been requested, in no uncertain terms, to present and make a case for **In the Moment**. A case that will establish convincing evidence of the *common* appeal, **In the Moment** has for the public at large. The case will be based on *mundanity*.

> Mundanity: Relating to or characteristic of the world. Characterized by the practical, transitory and ordinary: commonplace.

The concerns of day-to-day life. (*Merriam Webster's New Dictionary*)

In defense of *In the Moment*, its mundane allure ironically is its charm. It is the reality of the mundane—its attraction, its hook. I believe that "hook" rests in its *mundanity*, which is the intrinsic simplicity of *In the Moment*. Layered within are spiritual nuggets of precious insight into our human commonality—our ability to **Love.** Love is a universal *common* thread, a *common* hunger and thirst that connects one to another. Love is the human tapestry—*a gift.* **Love.** A spiritual and conscious attribute. It is our common sense that threads love into and out of this tapestry of life. Love, however, is *In the Moment!*

Common: Of or relating to a community, at large; public work for the good. Known to the community. Belonging to or shared by two or more individuals or things or by all members of a group. (*Merriam Webster's New Dictionary*)

An innate intuitiveness, a relative quality communicated by one's deeds made *common* for the good of all through one's *confessed love* . . . a *common* action. Especially those searching for the understanding of an *aha moment*—the epiphanies and revelations of life's paradoxical oxymorons.

This brings us to *sense*: the *common* vehicle or vessel, conveying intention—the purpose. The journey. The joy of being *In the Moment*. It is food for the hungry minds, for the soul thinkers. The written nutritional thoughts, articulating effectively, the power of the universal mind as a basis for one's actions and responses. For those searching insatiably, the *written Scriptures*, as well as for those searching hungrily in the literary marketplace, for the understanding and fulfillment of the *aha hunger*, *In the Moment* is the fulfillment. The epiphany and revelation of living life's paradoxical oxymoron, exposing the secret to the meaning of life *In the Moment*.

It is written . . . then marketed to be read and consumed for its relevancy, its *common sense* appeal, and to whomever is *In the Moment*. Peace. Love always . . . Mick E. Jones

ACKNOWLEDGMENTS

First and foremost, I want to acknowledge my beautiful, wonderful, patient, and loving wife, Sue. For without her in the light, I would not be here. *Hear me . . .* I would not be here! She is a source of strength, endurance, persistence, and forty-two marvelous years of marriage. She has no rival. She has no equal. She stands with me against all the adversities life can dish out and never complains, never puts me down, and always speaks truthfully. An integral part of a successful partnership in life and the Truth and the Way—Christ. Without which, I would not be here. You hear that now, don't you?

Next to my wife stands my son, Toren, my little boy—a gift—all grown up. My sun and my son. He is part of the light in my life, yet once he was my nemesis. It was from this frame that he inspired me to grow in stature, come to understanding and mature in ways I had never imagined. Without him, I would not be here. It was a lot to ask of a boy, yet he performed as a man when I was but a boy. The transformation was elevating, exciting, and beautiful.

I acknowledge him to the fullest with love, admiration, and respect.

Beyond the four walls and out in the garden stands a hedge comprised of many people who have been in, at, or near me when needed and when called on. They are my friends . . . even those friends for whom I pray ceaselessly—for they are within a hairsbreadth of vanishing into the black hole, out of which comes nothing. But, without them, I would not be here. *Hear this*: each person, be they family, friend, or otherwise, has sparked within me a greater understanding as to the meaning of my life! They helped me in creating **In the Moment** . . . for they are the *moment*. Every moment I stand, ready to leave on a journey near or far, they are there to remind me of my responsibility and mission in life.

Can you imagine that beyond all of these blessings stands one to whom goes all the glory and all the praise: **Our Father**! It is to him I acknowledge my life, my very existence, my heart which bursts with love, and these words, which I've penned to honor him, glorify him, and lift those of his flock who've fallen, as we all have, myself included, up and back onto the path home to him who created us, loves us, and knows each of us by name.

His Son, Christ Jesus, born out of love for all that lives, gave us his life for our salvation and rose again . . . yes, resurrected from the grave, to establish us as his adopted family. We, who have accepted and been *born again* into his eternal grace, have been adopted by **Our Father** into his heavenly home as his children. In turn, he has given us the opportunity to instill in our children his love, strength, mercy, and righteousness so that when called, we may stand before his throne and **hear**—mind you, *hear!*—him say, "Well done, my good and faithful servant."

But it doesn't end there. When Jesus Christ ascended into heaven forty days after his death upon the cross, he called upon his father—***Our Father***—to give us a helper . . . to give us truth and faith and understanding. He told the disciples to tarry in Jerusalem after his ascension so that they could be baptized in the Holy Spirit. The Holy Spirit of Jesus Christ, Son of God—***Our Father!*** From that day forward, we have been graced with his eternal and living love. All you do to access the Holy Spirit is believe with an unwavering heart in his permanence and presence as the only living God. In this way, you might become a willing vessel for his truth. Your faith must be strong, your eyes and ears open, ready to see and hear. There is no mistaking the Word of God, and to be sure, he provided us with the Holy Bible! Here, his inspired Word speaks loudly on all aspects of maturing a love that is unshakable and unbreakable for our Lord and Savior, Christ Jesus—***Our Father!***

I acknowledge him beyond measure. Thank you.

Mick E. Jones

INTRODUCTION

A moment—a scant sliver of time—into which the breath of life may be shared with another. One moment leads to another moment, and a string of moments creates *Time*. In time we see, we hear, we act, and we judge. We compare, we look for, we establish. Some of the time in excellence; some of the time in mediocrity. Each moment is important to the fullness of time. One moment poorly spent will inflict upon the remainder a taint hard to erase. A moment well spent will endue a lifetime of joy. Ultimately, it is one's life in all its deviations. The observations and the experiences openly shared and confessed in truth and spirit. *In the Moment It Is Written!*

In this moment, I have created a combination of events, thoughts, questions, reflections, and interactions that produce and give greater meaning and a deeper reverence for my personal relationship with God—Our Father. These influences have empowered me with a deeper perception of my purpose, *In the Moment*.

In other words, the experiences I enjoy every day have stimulated me to write down where the roots in my life are going. How to observe, engage, and participate. It is an examination of the crossing of the burning sands: going through the fire and then to give a written account. A statement of reasons that explains my conduct and how I have arrived at my *conclusions*. A living record in the form of the written word. My testament, ***In the Moment***, is a living proof of a covenant between God and the human race. The proof . . . the evidence: me! Now, the moment we are united in . . .

. . . is one moment of many moments—an authentic, firsthand record of the facts of a life lived as fully as I am able to comprehend—by grace. By living, by experiencing, by observing—then extracting and digesting the spiritual substances, the essences of all that has transpired into shape and form.

The insight of seeing beyond the visual effects of material things. Not saying we shouldn't have things, but they don't give us life. We have them because we are alive.

But! Do things really make life right or perfect for us—mentally, physically, or spiritually? Life is about living as opposed to being dead. Life is an interactive experience creating this reality we call *living*. That's why the quality of life for humans is precious and spiritually dignified by the total respect and reverential appreciation of every moment. To honor and to value the essence of our being. To be human! A great treasure and a deep responsibility—a noble purpose. To be human and to be alive.

And, sadly, I have seen this elegant privilege—a gift of God's grace go to waste. A political disgrace of church and sad state. The gift of grace—disappearing, fading, and eroding. We all lose face. It seems by design. A sign of the times. Just the revelation.

It's a day-to-day reality—***In the Moment***. Life is subtle and not so subtle. We are all apart of this degenerating cycle for we all fall short of "the glory." *It Is Written!* But thank God, there is not only hope—there is salvation! The light at the end of our tunnel of dark deeds where, by grace, we can experience the salvation of God's love, mercy, and forgiveness in a twinkling of an eye. ***In the Moment*** where truth and freedom reign supreme.

MICK E. JONES

Does it *take* a character to create compelling characters?

No, but it helps, and Mick E. Jones *is* one and has *plenty*—of character, that is.

An accomplished athlete, actor, author, singer, inspirational speaker, poet, and all-around fascinating talent, Mick E. is an amazing source for spiritual guidance of all kinds to all walks of life. His joie de vivre is infectious and should be required reading, viewing, or listening for the informed and inquisitive modern mind.

Mick E. Jones has a voice. And he speaks it often and to great effect. His trademark baritone always hides a smile and gives his readings or stories and characters extra life and flavor. Lucky Los Angelenos saw his one-man show *The Lounge Act* in 2011 at the Fifty-second Street Playhouse. And he's in that new Sony commercial too. His successful book *Cat Tales: Da' Real Pussy* is filled with his ruminations on the character of his neighborhood felines.

Boxing is a lifelong passion of Mick E., and you can catch him training another generation of fighters at his base camp at the Hollywood YMCA. Not content to just develop the physical body and coordination to its highest level, Mick E. also lectures before various groups, particularly students of all ages, with his inspirational message of positive thought expressed through his teachings, featuring his unique brand of poetry, hip-hop styling, and wry musings on life, liberty, and the pursuit of happiness. These appearances have become an institutional experience here in Los Angeles and other Southern California cities.

Once you've spent fifteen minutes with Mick E., life as you know it will change, guaranteed.

Sincerely,
Roy "Rogers" Odenkamp

MICK E. JONES

FROM BEYOND-THE GENIUS GOES ON: I CAN'T SEE SHIT

A spoken word CD from one of Hollywood's hidden talents, which bespeaks his love and respect for the late great Ray Charles.

CD Baby Price: $12.97

Who Is Mick E.?

I'm glad you asked. Mick E. is an *E*nigma. An element of surprise. Mick E.'s simple truths are heard in his humorous stories of social reflections. Mick E. speaks in the spirit of love. He will take you on an *E*volutionary journey within the divine purpose. An athlete, actor, and author of *Cat Tales: Da' Real Pussy* (www.amazon.com), you have probably seen Mick E. in numerous national commercials. You might recall him with Fred Williamson, "Hammer, I'm here." Mick E. has appeared with other notable actors such as James Earl Jones, Billy Dee Williams, and Courtney B. Vance in *Percy and Thunder*. Mick E. appeared in *Who's the Boss* and toured nationally with Shelly Garrett's *Living Room* in which he co-starred as Leonard. Mick E. also appeared in the off-Broadway cabaret play *Hey, Dad*. Mick E. is currently revising his one-man play *The Lounge Act* and his next book *Pieces of Peace*.

Now for the first time on cdbaby.com, Mick E. brings his spoken word talent to his audience. With his CD From Beyond-The Genius Goes On: I Can't See Shit, Mick E. brings his wit, irreverence, comic timing, and yes, genius, to the Genius of Soul, the late, great Ray Charles.

Why Ray? Good question! Actually, Ray chose me. That's the bottom line. I believe this. This belief is based upon my sister Nia Terry. She had solicited—no begged me—to come up with an idea that would make reading the Bible fun for kids. This is where Ray comes in. As I am reading aloud the passage "You walk by faith, not by sight," my voice commences to change. Then, speaking as if on its own, I was speaking as Ray with Ray as Mick E. I said, "Who is this?" The voice said, "Ray Charles." "What'd I say?"

I said, "Ray, how we going to get these kids to want to know the Word of God?" Ray said, "Like God, with love." A good example. It's the law. Of God's will. This be done for the good of his children. That for me was more than an epiphany. It was a connection to the social and spiritual side of Ray Charles. Beyond the Genius. And it is still going on—life after death. What a tribute. What a testimony. What an honor to be the vessel. What'd I say, "I Can't See Shit."

1. Close Your Eyes
2. Politricks
3. Can You Hear Me Now
4. What I Say
5. White Niggers
6. Nasty Dawg
7. Egghead Christian
8. Later Alligator
9. Speaking of James Brown
10. The News Isn't Good
11. Stevie Wonder Can See
12. Inspiration—Pro Choice
13. Dna
14. 911—Homeland Security

DEALING WITH . . . AMY

I n the beginning, this was originally supposed to be a follow-up to a letter, revisiting and clearing up a misunderstanding resulting from an earlier conversation I had with my niece. Because of certain mind-sets all ready in place, this *misunderstanding* bloomed into a conflict of interests.

As things developed along the way, this conversation became the focus of a growing lack of awareness and a belief in a misconception of what really took place. The time of reconciliation has arrived.

In the Moment became the forum that allowed a study of stated intentions, which highlighted clashes with hidden agendas. These intentions being modified by the "sins of the father" and recycled through "the mama's drama" revealed the true motivation.

It seems that with some people it is a family trait, and for others, it is a gender characteristic, which will be revealed through the following circumstances. This experience is a gem more precious than the Hope Diamond.

This *gem* is an accurate reflection of God's enlightened reason—a true insight of his love, forgiveness, and deep understanding of why we all fall *short of the glory* and our world a ball of confusion!

Preach on, rabbi! Preach on! 'Cause Jesus is alive and well. It's all n' da' family! When . . . when it is in the body of Christ. The Passion of Jesus!

My darling and precious niece *Amy* is really somebody special. She is very interesting, intelligent--academically speaking! She is beautiful, effervescent, charming, and a crafty *man-nip-u-lator*! Her personality radiates. It bubbles with glee and sparkles through her dark brown eyes.

She has very pretty eyes—they flash with joy and glare with the fire of anger, especially when she is upset. Then, you see the fury of a woman's wrath. More importantly, Amy is my niece! A wonderfully entertaining, well-traveled, educated person. Yet! Yet very narrow-minded and close-minded. Not surprisingly, she is a very opinionated person with points of view not necessarily shared by me.

It is the spiritual loveliness that graces her point of view, thereby saving our conflict from becoming a serious confrontation. Our face-off was declared "No foul, no harm." We saved face, **In the Moment**; however, the point I wish to convey is how I chose to deal with the Amy predicament. It came down to Amy's reactions to my choices of action, for there are no actions without reactions.

She insulted me—in my own home! She thought she had charmed me by manipulating me into thinking what she had made was a caring gesture supporting a close relationship, which did not exist! We are very different persons with two very different points of view.

First and foremost, Amy's tone came across as opinionated. This reaction revealed a preconceived concept that clashed with my own point of view. When all this is watered down, it translates to the bare fact that Amy and I are not only on different pages, but we are in two different *books of life.* Drawing from entirely two different references. Two distinct points of view.

This does not make for closeness. Respect, yes! Close? I don't rightfully know. I'll let the **readers** form their own conclusions. Read on . . .

Anyway, Amy's point of view is a very simplistic one. In fact, she wrote an after-the-fact letter in which she briefly explained her point of view. I'll call it Exhibit A. Here it is as I received it:

Dear Mick E.,

I was so sad to find out that you had left Saturday Evening without even saying, *Good-bye.* Although, I realized that I hurt your feelings on Thursday night, I thought that we were close enough to either talk it out there or find another way to fix the rift. I had hoped that my gift of flowers would help mend things, but I guess the daises didn't work.

When I arrived Thursday night, I was excited to see the entire Jones Family—something I always look forward to. And, I was thrilled to be able to share some champagne with you and discuss your manuscript. However, I also wanted to hear about Susan's successful completion of her course (the reason I brought the champagne), and about the wonderful job she is doing in the classroom. I began to feel frustrated because, as much as I love to hear your opinions, they seemed to be the only thing I could hear.

Your conversations are fascinating, but they tend to overwhelm whomever else has something to say.

I mentioned that I wanted to spend some time with my Aunt, because I felt that was the only way I was going to hear what was going on in her life. Mick, I would never want to hurt your feelings. Getting to know you again during the past two years has been a joy for me. I am sorry if I was insensitive in the way I broached the subject and I will try and be more feeling in the future. I do hope that the next time I visit, you will join Susan, Toren and I in some of our adventures and tell me directly if we need to talk something out.

All my love, Amy

Bravo! I mean give her a standing **O**! That was well put, and I am deeply impressed and touched. But sentiment isn't what I am here to uncover. I am trying to establish *a point of view*. Simultaneously, I am exploring motivations through close observation of behavior and looking for hidden agendas.

Now a written confession of *not a clue* as to the insulting of me by my niece—my own niece—is *unbelievable*! I understand that Amy is clueless; therefore, her point of view is understandable. Regardless of the fact that I have already pinpointed and satisfied my point of view. Arguing a case of *ignorance* is never an excuse, and it is never *bliss*. And neither is a narrow upbringing. So let's get down to the *nitty-gritty*!

If there is to be a true relationship, it must be founded on the solid ground of truth and clarity. The objective must have good intentions, even though the references are on different pages and from different books—the truth shall set you free! And the truth is, Amy is a fun person and a fund-raiser!

Yes! Amy was raising funds for her college—*Emerson* and, truth be told, going all across the country—like a big-time *evangelist* get'n dat' *moo-nay*! That's why she was here in Hollywood. **Money! Money! Money, honey!** Amy was here soliciting the rich and the famous—use'n her charm and motto: "You gotta have money, if you wanna get along wit' me! Money, honey!"

Oh, she has done Hollywood, Beverly Hills, the big studios. Met the stars of Hollywood. I'm not talking *stars*—*Hollywood Squares* stars nor PR stars keeping careers afloat. We are talking about *major players*.

Jane Fonda—Barbarella herself. Ted Turner—the Color Master. If it ain't colored by Ted Turner, *Da Master*, don't deal with it! Ted can't stand *black-n'-white*! Ironically, this is exactly the same thing Amy and I began to bump heads on—the black-and-white issue! In fact, it was Amy who called the shot when she said, "Mick E., life is not **ALL** black and white!"

That was so odd of Amy to say because I never, ever preface life as anything. I was referring to Ted Turner and rich and famous people with political aspirations, the lustful thirst and carnal hunger to wield power and be *masters of the universe*. To me, these fiendish moguls, like the government, are not to be trusted as sincere in their *giving*.

It's like when organized crime gives at the temple, mosque, synagogues, cathedrals, and the local church—I always remember who these givers are—and how they got what they gave. They have the mind-set of a merchant marine. A pirate—*a robber baron*—who don't give unless the return is greater in the end! Because they are the rich, famous, powerful, influential, affluent, shakers, makers and breakers, AND most are takers! They give fifty billion, and they get fifty times fifty back and . . . *som' mo!* These are the high rollers and not true givers.

Me saying this about the rich and powerful seemed to upset Amy. I won't say *upset*—*irritate* would be more to the point. I could hear the irritation and frustration as Amy restated, "Mick E, you make life too black and white. There are grays and other colors of life!"

Amy commenced to get a little uptight, so I tried to soften this *uppity tightness* by using the ole "tongue in

cheek" approach by saying, "Amy, maybe you're right. Life is not black and white. Maybe that's why Ted Turner colored all the black AND white films. But it's sort of odd, all the important documented papers are white, and the print, the important stuff, like the information, is Black."
Oops! Dere it iz . . . again. Oops . . . dere it iz!

But this conversation was just the tip of the iceberg. Then came the *Titanic* where our conversation would sink into verbal conflict, and Amy would amend her charming constitution AND deconstruct reconstruction. The South would rise again! Raising historical facts of life in which we sunk into *who's family mattered:* black or white, blues or grays? This constitutional amendment came to be legislated when Amy presented this scenario, saying, "Mick E, you don't think rich people can give and be sincere about helping the poor and hungry? The starving people of the world. And I am talking about black people in particular. And Ted Turner is sincere!"

At this point, Amy's constitutional demurrer switched up a notch. It wasn't quite as effervescent or bubbly; rather it was boiling! Amy was defending the rich and the famous with valor and with patriotic vigor. You could almost hear the drum and bugle corps playing "Glory! Glory! Hallelujah!"

Amy stood there looking like Betsy Ross, ready to design a new flag and stick it in my heart, because I had blasphemed against the rich and famous. From Amy's point of view, maybe, maybe, she was right. After all, she came to charm the rich and the famous. She's a fund-raiser—a *professional* fund-raiser—and very good at it!

When you think about it, a fund-raiser is a lot like a politician. They know how to kiss up. They are great actors, and like former movie stars, good actors become good politicians. And personally, I'm not fond of any of the political actors—stage, film, TV, or Oval Office. They're all some of the greatest fund-raisers, yet people are still *po' starving and hungry.* These Puff Daddies create problems, then pretend to solve them. They have buckets of money, yet toss out a few coins, saying, "It takes *mon-nay 2 make mon-nay.*"

Therefore, I cut them no slack. Whether white or black or gray! Or any other color! And that goes double for the Color Master himself—Mastuh Mr. Ted Turner. TBS. TNT. TMC. and all the rest of his T.S., and that goes for his son, Mr. T as well. What did I say that for?

This is when Amy so coldly and boldly said, "I want to talk with my aunt. That's what I came here to do! To talk to my aunt and my cousin. I'd love to hear your opinions and social philosophy some other time.

To really emphasize the break in viewpoint, she drove the point home laying it on me again, demanding, "Mick E.! I came to talk to my aunt!"

For me, it was there, ***In the Moment***, when everything clicked. I remember my eyes shuttering—*click! click!*—because it was like traveling back in time, to a time when Amy's mother and I almost had the same identical conversation. It was at 1209 Boylston Street,

Boston, Massachusetts—back in the '70s. I even had the conversation with Amy's grandmother, Peggy Sullivan. I had come full circle! All I was missing was Billy Preston singing "Willie It Go Round in Circles." Deja vu!

It was when the circle was the fullest that I knew the buck was gone. It had stopped here! Right this minute, and stop it did! And . . . it was so simple, so cool, and so, so very kind!

As I continued to reflect on the completion of my circle of life, I began to rub my hands in front of my face. Like I used to do when warming them after coming out of the cold back in New England! I blew on my hands. Because suddenly this moment had a real social and historical repetitious chill to it!

I looked at my Amy . . . slowly. I turned, and I squinted my eyes so as to really put this *In the Moment!* I had to really see if what I was hearing was what I thought it meant. I began to articulate my words. They came out of my mouth slowly, softly, and very deliberately. My words, their tones carried a deep spiritual concern. Their sounds rung in my ears as I heard myself ask, "Amy, do you have any idea—any clue—what that sounds like to me when I hear you say, 'I want to talk to my aunt'? 'That's what I came here to do.'"

I gave her a moment—a chance, so to speak, for it to sink in. The moment sank dramatically into an abyss. It turned out with Amy that nothing sunk in. While nothing went over Amy's head, nothing I was saying registered. *No thing. Nada! Zilch.* **Oops! Out ta' lunch.**

No matter how I would state it, restate it, use another scenario, the same results! Amy was clueless. And it would become more apparent as I continued this line of thought. It came to a head when I remarked, "Personally, Amy, I don't give a darn about Ted Turner, Ike, Tina, or Jane Fonda Barbarella Turner.

"What I care about, Amy, is do you have any idea how 'I want to talk to my aunt' hits my ear? What it feels like to me?

"Do you realize that in your thirty years of life I've known you, I have personally seen you roughly five times. That's in thirty years! And I guarantee in your thirty years, we have maybe, just maybe a paragraph of meaningful conversation.

"Amy, you have spent both quantity and quality times with your aunt during the past thirty years. In fact, it's roughly two years since you were out here, and you and yo' aunt yakety-yaked it up a-plenty! You dominated and dictated that evening, much as you are doing now! You are a lot like yo' mama! Ya' know? And I love both of y'all."

This was when I was introduced to the Amy law—and like Marsha Clarke, Amy dropped her brief on me.

"Mick E.," she said very cordially and so charmingly. Her voice having a professional edge to it as she informed me that she and her husband used Amy's law if they couldn't agree. Then it was agreed that they would agree not to disagree and move on to another topic. That's *the Amy's law.*

Now Amy informs me that the law dictates that we move on—like change the topic. Amy stated the law stipulates we change the topic to *I want to talk to my aunt!*

Oh! and it was **In the Moment** I understood the translation of the Amy law. It was very simple. The law stipulates clearly if Amy can't win, one must agree not to disagree with Amy's point of view, and then one changes the topic. No matter as to my personal trial and tribulation, Amy's law rules, and *I must shut up!*

Now Amy talks with her aunt without transgression of the law. *Case closed!* Which was her stated purpose for being there in the first place. In OUR home! That's as real as it gets. I'm down with that! No transgression here—Amy's da' law!

While this law was sinking into my mind—my intelligence scanner—Amy charmingly smiled, poured me a glass of champagne, and proceeded to talk with her aunt. Clear cut! The case was closed. ***Oops, dere it iz!***

Naturally, after finishing the drink and being the consummate gentleman as Amy is a lady, I followed *pro-to-col!* Drink finished, I left and went to a friend's *club*, which is the party room behind his house. His wife refers to us as the *the party train.* Well! We sho' par-tayed. Big time with big fun. It was just what I needed! A FUN-d-raiser. Looking back, if Amy would have given me a chance, I was going to bring her with me, but no, she had to talk to her aunt.

Hey! She was on a mission! Mission accomplished. I can respect that! The funny part about all this Mission

Accomplished quest is Amy's motivation or intentions to talk with her aunt, which was to hear what was going on in her aunt's life.

And here is the contradiction. How can one be interested in a person's life—in this case her aunt's—and not give a damn about her aunt's husband? A very intricate and delicious part of her aunt's life, just short of God. Praise da' Lord. I don't think y'all heard me. Praise da' Lord!

All this makes for a very interesting twist in dealing with Amy. That's Amy's written version of what took place at 1915 in Hollywood—in the new millennium.

I mean the incongruity and failure of Amy to mention any of these incidents, now presented as facts from my viewpoint, must be weighed fairly for a just hearing—by the reading!

You, as the **reader**, must weigh with an open mind to remain emotionally aloof, as it would bias your joy and ability to comprehend Exhibit A: *The* Letter and Exhibit B: The Contents and Details of My Point of View, which makes the letter of Amy's law pale in comparison, shallow in light of the truth, the whole truth, to prevail in its entirety!

Come on, folks. If you cut out all this "good stuff" that dealing with Amy has revealed, you have nothing left—just puffery! I guess that's the gray area of life that Amy is always referring to. As for hurting my feelings, she didn't hurt my feelings. She insulted me! *Duh!* For instance, the following day Amy called and told her aunt, "I want to take the Joneses to dinner."

I thought that was real cool. A nice political move. Smooth Amy! Then Amy's aunt informed me how the evening would proceed—we would all go to dinner, and then Amy's aunt said, "After dinner, I, Amy's aunt, and Toren, Amy's number one cousin, will accompany Amy, our relative—not yours—to Amy's hotel by special request. And there will be no sudden intrusion or unexpected surprise visit by the likes of you!

Wow! When I first heard that, it sounded all right. I mean Sue really didn't say *it* the way I wrote *it*; the writing has more of a *true bite*. But we're not talking about the truth—not here. We're talking about *man-nip-u-lation* of the truth. Now the partial truth of Amy's brief regarding her written confession of innocence and ignorance as to how she hurt my feelings—she pleaded nolo contendere on all charges.

I'm not charging Amy with ignorance. And she didn't hurt my feelings. She insulted me! That's the charge. Can we all agree on that? Now her aunt, my wife, and my son—Amy's number 1 cousin—have become her coconspirators solely because they're Amy's relatives. Bingo! That's when the click went off in my head—*click*! And I began to speak, "If we all are supposed to be FAMILY, I can go to dinner. But I can't go to Amy's. Don't even think of it! So y'all go to Amy's, and I'm dropped off at home. Alone!" What's wrong wit' dis' picture? I know what's wrong with the sound of it!

Click! Click! Click! My head is click'n 'cause that was da bomb and the last straw! *Boom!* Now it's Columbo time. I had to go to my closet and get my wrinkled Basil Rathbone/Sherlock Holmes trench coat and put in on! I got to! You know, Columbo Holmes! This is a heavy investigation. Let the proceedings begin:

Aha, Sue, Amy's aunt and my wife. Toren, our son, and Amy's number 1 cousin—the two of you, if my understanding is clear—both of you are going to Amy's after dinner. But first y'all gonna dump me. Right, homies?

After the dump, Amy's aunt and her number 1 cousin will continue with Amy, the fund-raiser of the rich and famous, continue cruising on to Amy's four-star—almost in Beverly Hills—hotel and go up to her suite and hang out for a while. Then come home! Right?

Sue and Toren, now Amy's insurrectionists and renegade/turncoats, stood there before me posturing and puffed up. Puffed with pride, they answered in unison almost in a song did their words ring out, "Amy wants us, not you."

This time the click snapped. Everything fell into place for me as I said, "Cool! It looks like the DNA is deeper than I thought! So! Guess who won't be coming to dinner?"

As I began to conclude my point of view, I added a brief letter to Amy explaining my actions. It was a very simply stated letter and went right to the point as to why I wouldn't be coming to dinner. It read as follows:

Amy,

   I'm not good at tokenism in the guise of family-ism. Thanks for your invite. But no thank

you! You can save the whales, save the pygmies, and
you can save your cordial charming insults, which are
starting to take their toll.
    Mick E.

Amy, ever so smooth—did I mention clever and oh! *so slick*—tried to smooth over the lumpy insults by bringing me some *DAZE-IES*. I don't think so! I guess Amy figured it always worked on the *Brady Bunch*. Perhaps she can work it on *Sanford and Son*. What da' hell, bro! Amy is very game and very funny.

It's funny that Amy in her short correspondence and amnesiac state of mind or, as the mental experts say, *state of selective memory,* fails to mention any of these historical events in Exhibit A: The Letter. It's like withholding evidence or obstruction of justice—the truth! The American Way. United we stand, and Amy claims to want to go on an adventure with me? If this isn't an amazing adventure of reality, what is? They should close Disneyland, like ***now***!

Last but not least, it is with this final submission that I will throw myself on the mercy of you, the readers.

Amy is absolutely correct. We did discuss my man-u-script. If you call this a discussion of the manuscript. Amy poured me a glass of champagne saying, "Mick, I can't really discuss your manuscript. Because I just started reading **IT**! I was going to bring it, but I forgot. Silly me! **Oops.**"

Smile and charm as she then changed the topic and started talking to her aunt. Well, I hope this clears things up for Amy.

. . . And no, Amy, you're not insensitive. You are sort of premeditative—in a harmless, sweet way. It's a mind-set syndrome. The Amy agenda. Amy's way or no way.

I'm glad you don't sell Amway, or I'd have an apartment full of lovable bullshit.

Bottom line: Who cares? I love ya and thanks for the memories. It's all good. The truth will set you free.

PS Amy, I left without saying good-bye to you because I already had permission from your aunt to leave. Which left you where you wanted to be—with yo' aunt. It's all good.

Peace,

Uncle Mick E.

Religion: The Mask of Satan

Why is religion losing?

With so many of the world religions, each of which supposedly supports God and claims to be doing God's will, with so many subscribers to the institution of love—God's universal law—*why is religion losing?*

Also, how could so many alleged God-loving followers be so unloving? How could these same followers do the most heinous, hateful, shockingly evil, and most abominable acts in the name of the loving God of the universe. Religion appears to express itself with a lot of *anti-God* behavior. *Whazz up wit' dat?*

The history of religion—past, present, and heading into the future—seems not only contradictory of God's will but has become mentally imbalanced and emotionally unstable when it comes to performing true acts of *love*. The law of God's will is to *love*. Not being done—*off wit' yo' head!*

This can be seen in religious circles all around the world. *Som'em wrong wit' dez' folks!* They are really queer, as in being questionable folks of God. Perverted men/women doing what they think is the will of God. They seem empty and lack the substance of God. Sort of like counterfeit money. An army of spiritually unfulfilled followers killing each other in the name of the one true living God of love. God's will is not being done. *Oh God!*

Religion, according to the world, has become a game of deceit. A most deceptive spiritual masquerade designed to confuse God's children—even the Elect. This is politically correct, yet all of it falls short of the *glory of God.*

Today's religion is a spiritual masquerade of evil. Organized religion is an evil force designed to destroy people's faith in the name of the true living God. God is our spiritual government, the one to whom we turn to within. These are the components of our spiritual DNA—the divine natural anointed laws of God! This is love! A vibrant, authentic spirit! A light that radiates from inside the followers who are believers who walk by faith and not by sight—as do the world religions. Religion is a charade of diabolical masqueraders of a God who loves to kill in the name of a God who loves to love. *Hmmm . . .* ponder that for a moment.

Religion: *the anti-God!* So you know they ain't in the body of Christ—the one who came for **ALL** and *loved* **ALL.** He was about his Father's will. *Love* is the foundation of God's law. The foundation of peace. The Passion of Christ. Nevertheless, these alarming conditions come as the church is being infiltrated by the enemies of God. Why? Because God's children don't love naturally. They don't have the courage to stand up for God, and when and if they do, it's wrong. It's an institutional reflex created by men so that they may rationalize the following of false prophets, teachers, ministers, as well as condone the actions of spiritually ill-prepared parents. World religion is a spiritual placebo, a Pavlov syndrome, a conditioned reactive reflex resulting from following self-appointed and self-ordained false shepherds who not only don't recognize the truth—they hate it! *Hooray for Hollywood*, the city of lost angels—angel less. Plenty of stars—alas, no angels. Hell's angels . . . ***Snap! Snap!***

The world community's political environment is ready to condemn religion. Contempt for the world's religions has set the stage by using state-sponsored tools of corruption to disenfranchise the spirit of Christ's church and create an environment ripe for war. The state now holds the bag and is ready to drop the bomb at any moment. This sorry mess comes out of the spirit of the left and the right, conservative, and liberal. Gay. Never straight or truly happy. The king is da' queen. The money is funny, and Wall Street falls. State, the pot. Call'n church the skillet black! In a White House. Hail 2 da' chief!

All means a people who are disconnected from humanity—from being human. They have been scattered to the ends of the earth, and they *all* are becoming cyber cloned—a spiritually dead and hopelessly misled unity. These same people, same mask—left, right, grandparents, parents, sons, daughters, and kinfolk of every persuasion—compose the whole in which this cancer festers. The pseudo-psycho religious leaders, believers, and followers of church and state are but the mask of Satan being revealed. Satan has commenced to unmask its evil face! *Peekaboo!* Gotcha! The world . . . *a ball of confusion.*

Without the spirit of the truth and *repentance by true confession of evil,* left, right, or anything will remain just that—**evil!** The same face, the same problem. A church and state still politically correct yet in severe denial—mimicking humanity. Justifying themselves with the only excuse available: "The devil made me do it!" The sheep, the Lord's flock, have been hypnotized, brainwashed, politically cultivated into floundering followers. Like Lemmings, they fall one after another into the abyss. Faster and faster, they move in the wrong spiritual direction. **Truly a 9/11!** *Religion of da' terrorist!* Can you feel it now?

The agony versus the ecstasy: the pleasure of pain, the hope of failure, the acceptance of death, and the rejection of life has confused, frustrated, depressed, and spellbound most followers to the point they don't see it coming *In the Moment* of *truth!* The effort to blind the follower by removing God's will from their lives has surpassed all expectations . . . the *dumbing* down gambit has paid off. People are blind, deaf, and dumb!

The scam grows daily in the effort to remove God's will from believer's lives. For example, eliminating God from the Pledge of Allegiance, the fight to disallow the public posting of the Ten Commandments, no praying without ceasing. No praying, period. Except National Prayer Day—one day. Amen!

This is the outcome for the righteous who know what to do but wait for someone else to actually step up and **do** his will. In place of the righteous, now we have clones, look-alikes who are mere deceptions cleverly deployed to assume control of our spiritual government. Evil in high and low places.

Lost is the truth! This precious freedom *LOST*! It's not to be found in America. Certainly not in our schools. How do **you** keep hope alive? *The substance of* **faith,** the evidence unseen. ***Oops, all gone!*** Walk by faith according to MTV?

God consciousness is no longer vital or vibrant in our minds, our hearts, our spirits, our homes, and all the places that give life to the beautiful, loving laws of God's will. Mainly, the children of God. The fruit of the womb. God's reward is being deceived by religion, the *mask of Satan*. Hail Mary and damn the torpedoes. ***Boom!*** *Off with their heads! Cyberspace baby killers!*

The name of the game is SATAN! If we don't own up to it and call it by the name God gave it, then this great deceit of the satanic infiltrated church and sad state will succeed in reshaping the American nation. The land we love. Our liberties are already being eroded, corrupted, stolen, and annihilated. It's hell! No! I won't go!

Evil religions—church and state infiltrators! Traitors! *Infidels!* They've turned away God's love and have invaded and corrupted our soil. They have planted worthless seeds of materialism, allowing nothing real, nothing lovely to grow. We have become a nation of buildings dedicated to destruction and decorated with lies, peopled by prisoners of death, authorized by the sad state, and sanctioned by Satan. Now . . . the church!!

The wages of sin . . . **death**. The occupation . . . **evil**. The gain . . . the **world**, and the loss . . . your **soul**. Revisionism has rampantly destroyed the faith we once held as sacrosanct. It all seems futile, given the lying undermining world religious values, which are aimed at restructuring all of God's gifts of life. Remade to fit evil's ill-lusion. We "ill'n" **in silence**. Reality TV for the blind. A deaf jam. **Aha—*In the Moment!***

Illusion is all that it is because God in the person of his Son, Christ Jesus, as our Savior and by his grace **is for real, Is real,** and will not counter man in his willingness to be duped. If one believes, trusts, and acts on the will of God's law of love, one can be saved by the truth of God's word and set free . . . from the church and sad state of Satan's organized world religious mask! It's the light of God's loving grace that will expose the darkness in religion and who or what is behind the *mask*. An Un-united state in a God we cannot trust. Why? Is Christ divided?

The following documented information will give you the answer. Fasten your church and state seat belts: *Religion is the mask of Satan*. From the very beginning, it has been the objective of Satan to have his power based in the pews of churches around the world. They are his "heavy hitter" team. They who leave on Sunday afternoons to deliver Satan's message around the world by declaring their sinful lives as righteous and their hypocritical words as truth. They perform daily in public as men and women of stature and respect. They are the people who have been exalted above ALL others and idolized and sanctified as role models and rabbis. These are the children of God who now live in glass houses, worshiping in cathedrals with Satan's transgressions artfully illuminated by the light of the morning sun. But wait! No **SON**-light!

They are Satan's greatest asset in his effort to undermine the Word of God and pry open the ark of trust God has placed on our hearts. That place in our being where he can commune with the believer has been identified by eminent scholars and prominent theologians and is now under attack. The men and women who are respected experts in the field of historical theological research and know everything you want to know about everything, especially with reference to the human condition, which is the central theme of Satan's manipulation of men and woman, boys and girls. *Gotcha!*

This unmasking of religion was declared by *Mr. and Mrs. Know-it-all.* The people who are well respected and considered by their peers to be experts. The gurus of life—the heavies. The people said to possess deep spiritual and intellectual knowledge and understanding, with extraordinary power and ability to define and validate the origin of man and God.

They have traced the roots of religion down to where there are no further roots and have declared that further research will be necessary to determine if the empty void can be said to be related to the concept of nothing and zero.

Boy! They really get off on this kind of stuff. They marvel and revel and delight in themselves. Powerful men and women, the editors who work up a sweat carving life out of rocks, riffraff, and garbage, turning around and declaring this to be the origin of man!

Mothers and fathers, take heed of the powerful draw these self-ordained parental doctors—men and women, great scientists and ministers—who claim to have all known understanding. Beware of their unequivocal admonitions, declarations, truths that are Unfounded and Unbelievable, preaching Unconditional love from the pulpit and pews of religion. Hell is being raised! It has been officially written and consummated that *religion is the mask of Satan.* A political agenda! *Hello!* The sputtering and spewing of half-baked, scripturally wrong sentimentalities wrapped up in prophetic insights will only deceive and delude. They can only take the believer into bondage and away from the light. Out of communion with God and into Satan's prerecorded message that converts God's word into pathetic homilies and catchy, feel-good phrases, which have no meaning in the light of God's grace and infinite love. They have no meaning in the heart of believers unmoved by these academic double speakers pushing their brand of balm onto newly *born-again* Christians. *The new Jew.* The seed of Abraham, the Just.

The truth is that religion and so-called Christianity is a spiritual facade created to delude the believer and hide God's true will. God's good will and mercy are being trampled underfoot by crowds of pleasure seeking men, women, and children wanting more of the *good life*. The gift we received when Jesus took our sins to the cross is being tokenized and diluted into nothing more than another IMAX blockbuster! Religion is a front for Satan—*the mask* is fooling more and more people every day. Many are called, yet few will come. **Self-righteousness is never right or godly.**

It is written:

Beware of false prophets, who come to you in sheep's clothing, but inwardly they are ravenous wolves.

Matthew 7:15

For false Christs and false prophets will rise and show great signs and wonders to deceive, if possible, even the elect.

Matthew 24:24

Now I urge you, brethren, note those who cause divisions and offenses, contrary to the doctrine which you learned, and avoid them.

Romans 16:17

This is the researched and documented factual proof that God's children—men, women, mothers, and fathers are divided and conquered by Satan who, through careful cultivation, polarizes the politics of church and sad state. Masked by Satan's institutional false doctrine of conflict and contradiction.

Thus, perhaps, this is why religious groups always point the finger at one another. Fingering each other as evil and the false face of God. After all, it takes one to know one. And when they tire of fingering you—they give you the anointed finger. Flashing 'n flipping it all the while cursing in the manner of their hypocritical master: *the Beast Man!*

If that don't get your attention, they attack you in the name of their real god, Satan! Wearing the mask of their daddy's religious BS.

Attacking and retaliating religiously. Going to war! Literally raising up hell! *"The wages of sin is death."* That's why war is hell. It's a religious, self-righteous damnation to your soul. Just listen to any veteran of these religious and politically motivated church and sad state, "UNHOLY WARS, against Almighty God." A political agenda! It's the AM-bush of principality—Bush-shit. ***Gotcha!*** And . . . you have got to be a world religious mask-wearing political devil to K-ILL. Killing in the name of THE ALMIGHTY and universal God who commanded, **"Thou shalt not kill."** Many wars have been fought, and many men have died in the name of **religion**; but no one has died in the name of **God**, the one and only true God, ***Our Father,*** who created us and has sustained us regardless of our foolishness, except for One . . . **his Son, Christ Jesus**. He died in the name of God to save our sorry asses from hell in perpetuity. And Satan suffered his worst defeat ever.

I'm really enjoying this exposure by the experts who have equated religion and Christianity being the best example of world religious political mask wearing. Oddly enough, the Christian mask is the face of Jesus. The resurrected Christ. The mask—a false face worn so long, it has developed a white life of its own. Resurrecting itself from the false prophet or anti-Christ. A religious political state of mind now, God, the church, and state of Satan world religion, a political agenda of hell. **Gotcha!** It's a dead issue—the wages of sin! The burning bush of Satan.

Accordingly, the experts learned the mask wearers believe they're never wrong. Nor at fault. It's always the other false face who is at fault. It's like the pot calling the skillet black or snow white calling snowflakes **tar baby.** Name-calling, a serious stumbling block of church and sad state. The mask of world religion, a deception of political principality. Spiritually, *a ball of confusion.* Temptations forever! It's like football—an ENRON!

Take heed that no one deceives you. "For many will come in my name, saying, I am the Christ and will deceive many" (Matthew 24:5).

> For false Christs and false prophets will rise and show
> great signs and wonders to deceive, if possible, even
> the elect.
>
> Matthew 24:24

It's obvious that for the follower, religion isn't an easy adventure. Especially for the so-called Christians or those supposedly who are following Christ. *Trick or treat!* Church and state—so neat. Politically sweet. Spiritually, it might be a sour grape. Is Christ divided? I repeat, **you walk by faith,** not by religion! ***Aha, In the Moment!***

Christianity has been divided and cut mo' than bad street cocaine, and this division affects people's **Faith,** opening the door to evil! We all can be deceived, especially if you were taught by the false prophets whom you thought were *2-legit.* **Gotcha!** And this goes double for the experts and their research. Ain't that a twist. Chester **IS** da' molester—a priest! God have mercy!

I'm not one to judge; therefore, I did some research of my own. I researched the Scriptures, which revealed those who live by faith, they search the Scriptures in truth and spirit **and will know the truth!** They will not accept or follow the deception of any religious mask nor its false doctrine. This understanding will aid in your freedom to experience a true spiritual reality. The very reward God offers but that religious, church, and state experts say gets in the way of the truth. This shit is real and very fun-kay!

How? They closely control the dissemination of information. In that way, they edit, revise, and reverse what you are allowed to know. Then dictate what's politically correct. This is a religious media, a published ritual of church and state. The great impostor—*THE MASK* or the shroud of Jesus! False PR traffickers: www.satan.net

The mask of religion for many is the face of Jesus. The false Jesus, the mean spirit behind Satan's flag waving, patriotic, self-righteous crusaders who are killing in his name and worshiping behind a godly mask we cannot trust. Soon, it leads you to ground zero with the once-hated police and soon to be hated again—*your heroes!* This is why the victim always becomes the victimizer like a priest, minister, rabbi, president, pope, or the police. Y'all get my drift? This is why your Bill of Rights leads to civil wrongs. Evil marches on! And it resides in low and high places. *God have mercy.* **Forgive *us* for we know not.**

According to expert reports and the intervention of insights reflected through the love of God using me to throw it out into the world in writing, it seems and appears what has been filtered out to me through enlightened awareness is the fact that all of the world's organized religions church and states, by virtue of their political power, are ruining the world through false prophecy and have over twenty-one centuries reduced the living God's true spiritual laws of the universe into some fictitious metaphysical ritual. A facade of the unholy mask, an invention of their warped imagination as opposed to existential revelation for peaceful planetary coexistence. One people. One purpose. Who love to do the will of the true and universal God. To love . . . it's the law!

That's the word on the street today. The general law and plan of God's will. A universal "love ye one another." Unfortunately, I'm not referring to the plan of the real God. I am referring to *the mask*—the overt organizing and practice of world religion. A system of negations of God's will. Preaching pacifism while enacting an unholy crusade through terrorism. Independently constructing a financial edifice called *church, temple, mosque, glass cathedrals.* You name it, they got it! And they can afford it. Flying in their own jet planes.

Yes, the sky lords of world religion, churches, and sad state, also known as *the masketeers,* can affect one's personal relationship with God. Declaring mysteries in the church when they are heavily involved in the politics of hell. Hell being carried out through false teachers and preachers, rabbis, priests, ministers who are all *born again* in the spirit of their father, Satan, the liar and deceiver, the creator of the mask. A significant sign of intellectual fraud—AI or artificial intelligence. The religious myth has been exploded and exposed. Tithing and taxing out of the same plate. Gotta go! Good God! Hit me! *I'm in the Book of James . . . James Brown, that is!*

It is difficult for religious folks to grasp or accept the aforementioned. Because they have been culturally and institutionally brainwashed, morphed through spiritual seduction. Corrupted, they are now patriots and worshipers of the mask. Instead of submission to the Divine Creator, the one God, and obedience to God's law—to love the laws of God—they seek feel-good religion. *It's the drug of the day!* Unconditional love.

Follow pseudo-religion, the political corruption of Satan's degenerate right wing or left wing—Marxist, Socialist, Communist all rolled into a religious democracy ready to be *Hindu'd, voodoo'd, or you-hoo'd.* It's a meal over the top in calories, low in protein, rich in fats, bleached of minerals, and having no vitamins so that afterward you feel like you want to go out and puke, then die, preferably in the street. Gotta be low maintenance!

FAITH IN GOD . . . OR?

This leaves the followers of **the mask** spiritually trapped, sexually confused, and always sexually abused. The consequences of this entrapment, while in such a pseudo-religious conflict, seduces the spiritual desire into being fulfilled through sadism, masochism, and incest. Religiously sexually active. Free to FU—*praisin' da' Lord.*

Sin is in, it's *ab-fab* religious people transformed into Queer as Folks. *Wazz up, Bud-Wiser? It's Miller time.* The perforated high life tap'n into the Rockies. Then knock'n da' boots, screaming! Good booty hole! A priest gives you da' *"ben-a-dick-shun." ***Oops, dere it is!*** Praise da' lawd! Hail Mary a.k.a. Pope Francis.* Snap, snap! *Circle, gon' girl.*

After all, these were the freaked-out, perverted religious people who persecuted Jesus, who is *the way, the truth, and the life.* These people persecute you today, if you're really into the oneness of Christ, fighting the good fight of faith. The passion of Jesus, *born again* with compassion, the new Jew! Jews, Gentiles, and others who are God fearing and Christ minded are persecuted by people of religion!

The faithful must stand strong. The just who live by faith, walk in faith, and act in faith and trust in doing the will of God Almighty, *Our Father, the one and only true God,* are unafraid to call it like it is. Friday the thirteen / nightmare on Elm St. www.Vatican.come

Religion: The Mask of Satan—the god we cannot trust! The church and state mystery of spiritual political schizophrenia. Bush and the Beast, neither flesh nor blood. It's the *mask of principality,* worn by everyday people in high and low places. Scary, huh? Religion is a cult, which has been transformed into a tool of misinformation and false values. The masquerade is over! You never know what will be the stimulus to trigger a thought.

It's always something. One's viewpoint is never *nothing.* Nothing is the absence of something. Yet in the heart of a faith-based person, no thing is the absence of clutter. For what is faith but the absence of sight. Sight in the common sense. What we see is not always what we get. Therefore, worldly views and opinions must be based on something. Behavior is established through the exposure to the world's viewpoint. Therein rests the dilemma. The world moves one way, then another, creating conflict and confusion, yet God never moves. He remains outside of the *Ball* of Confusion. Those held in the grip of *the mask* are at risk of losing their soul because their views are not of the Lord, but of our world. What good is it? To God . . . for one to gain the world. It's the world's point of view.

Now our viewpoint—oh, say can you see my point? Will you view it? Can you hear me now? That's how faith comes. Right or wrong, good or evil. Ironic, huh? *I heard that!* **Now!** *Can you hear me?*

Faith is belief at its core. Faith comes before actualization. Faith overrides any other consideration. Once you have taken into consideration this or that or some other THING, you now believe some *THING*. Belief is an outgrowth of faith. Having faith in our Lord and Savior Jesus Christ is also belief. For God made Jesus for us to establish our faith. Before him, there was only faith and the miracles God performed in order to establish his kingdom on earth. But when Jesus Christ came, it became faith transformed in believing that he is the Messiah. Now what does the mask of Satan do but hide behind the veil of religion and cultural politics. Satan is a gutted fish.

Faith is the foundation of our spirituality. It is the substance of which our souls are made wonderfully and eternally. It is the life of *hope,* our confession, a living testimony. The evidence of the unseen!

> *For we walk by faith, not by sight.*
> 2 Corinthians 5:7

> *Faith is the substance of things hoped for, the evidence of things not seen.*
> Hebrews 11:1

And I heard it was a gift. A gift of God. Not a gift of one's thinking. Because one's thinking is subject to change according to one's thoughts. According to Scriptures, that ain't the Lord.

For I am the Lord, I do not change; . . .

Malachi 3:6

For my thoughts are not your thoughts, nor are your ways my ways, says the Lord.

Isaiah 55:8

And that's what this writing is all about . . . Helping a dear friend transform—to change gears, to set a new way, to hear a new word—and open her eyes to the beauty of the very life lifting her up each morning and putting her to rest each night. To renew her thought process on things that are of God. She seems to have a lot of conflict and irony within her faith. About what? About how God has instructed us to be in our faith journey with him *and* how to truly believe, trust and rely on God, in the person of Christ Jesus, by allowing his grace, judgment, and mercy to be active in our lives. This is a stumbling block.

Bottom line: with faith, keep it *simple, Simon!* Get the E-go out! Let go of pride!

Pride goes before destruction, and a haughty spirit before a fall.

Proverbs 16:18

Woe to those who are wise in their own eyes, and prudent in their own sight!

Isaiah 5:21

All of this writing is about a change of heart and mind of a person, a person very dear to *Our Father* and to me. She struggles with the reality of true faith and the purity of the spirit upon which faith is conceived. To be stress free, yet she is stressed and in bondage to ignorance of the laws that govern faith.

For the laws of faith are not temporal but spiritual. If the spirit is disconnected, then like a phone line, you can't get through to God and get the encouragement of his blessing and understanding. Though my friend is thoughtful, intelligent, not lacking in cognitive ability, is aware of her surroundings, and is above all, brilliantly gifted in several artistic and business disciplines, she nonetheless is blind and deaf to the real music, the real art, the real business of God and his Son, Christ Jesus. No, worldly ignorance is not the issue. It's ignoring and refusing to take literally what God's purpose is for those claiming to be *faithful and just!* The just who live by faith, not their own interpretations of faith, but according to the will of God, whose burden is light and not a struggle or an emotional roller-coaster of pride and ego.

But if you do not forgive, neither will your Father in heaven forgive your trespasses.

Mark 11:26

For if you forgive men their trespasses, your heavenly Father will also forgive you.

Matthew 6:14

But love your your enemies, do good, and lend, hoping for nothing in return; and your reward will be great, and you will be sons of the Most High. For He is kind to the unthankful and evil.

Therefore be merciful, just as your Father also is merciful. Judge not, and you shall not be judged. Condemn not, and you shall not be condemned. Forgive, and you will be forgiven.

Luke 6:35-37

Now may our Lord Jesus Christ himself, and our God and Father, who has loved us and given us everlasting consolation and good hope by grace, comfort your hearts and establish you in every good word and work.

2 Thessalonians 2:16-17

Take my yoke upon you and learn from me, for I am gentle and lowly in heart, and you will find rest for your souls. For my yoke is easy and my burden is light.

Matthew 11:29-30

My darling friend is suffering with unforgiveness. She can't forgive another person who had slighted, offended and angered her. Betrayed over something quite trivial. Both are confessed believers of Christ. The light of enlightened reasoning, yet both are caught in the self-righteousness of anger. The product of pride. And the fallout is detrimental to their faith and service to the Lord. Pride is a hedge against grace.

> *But I say to you, love your enemies, bless those who curse you, do good to those who hate you, and pray for those who spitefully use you and persecute you, that you may be sons of your Father in heaven; for He makes His sun rise on the evil and on the good, and sends rain on the just and on the unjust.*
>
> Matthew 5:44-45

> *There is no fear in love; but perfect love casts out fear, because fear involves torment. But he who fears has not been made perfect in love. We love Him because He first loved us.*
>
> 1 John 4:18-19

> *Cast your burden on the Lord, and He shall sustain you; He shall never permit the righteous to be moved.*
>
> Psalm 55:22

> *The Lord also will be a refuge for the oppressed, a refuge in times of trouble.*
>
> Psalm 9:9

> *Peace I leave with you, My peace I give to you; not as the world gives do I give to you. Let not your heart be troubled, neither let it be afraid.*
>
> John 14:27

Bottom line—*the final analysis*—the conclusion or closure to this spiritual conflict . . . a dilemma of our will/ego versus God's good will for our inner peace. The peace within the body of Christ when we truly have spiritual peace of mind. We pass the peace for we are *born-again* peace bearers. We keep the peace, and we let go and let God's will be done!

A LECTURE

I was told I lecture. Oddly enough, even though I don't consider following a line or course of conversation with what I feel is a proper response stimulated by a statement that comes to a logical conclusion or reasonable deduction is the grounds for an indictment of lecturing. I don't lecture, do I? Nonetheless, I can understand and except the jacket of lecturer/preacher. It's a sort of backhanded compliment as to the wisdom of God's clarity. I would compare the clarity to a *litmus test*—the Holy Spirit within me tends to draw out and reveal the truth of the spirit behind the personality I am dealing with. It helps explain why they react or overreact to the spirit within me. It's all good.

> *My brethren, count it all joy when you fall into various trials, knowing that the testing of your faith produces patience.*
>
> James 1:2-3

When my faith is tested, it is strengthened, broadened, deeply enriched. God is edified, and my wisdom increased and the writing fuller, the love more pure, the enlightenment simplified with kindness. The revelation of God's mercy and forgiveness revealed, *for we all fall short of his glory.*

Let the lesson begin on why this whole existence we call life is a school. Son-day school, if you are a true believer in Christ Jesus, the resurrected spirit of God's love and protection of our fragility. Especially for those sincerely seeking, those looking inwardly, diligent to connect to the peace, the good will, the walking and talking by faith. A confessional as a living testimony is being transformed by God for their repentance on a daily basis, so stay *In the Moment!* and overcome the world by all means necessary in Christ Jesus. Through the teaching and example taught to you in the spirit of truth, guided by the Holy Spirit and heard by the continuous hearing, receiving, but mostly the doing God's will. It is called obedience.

Obey! Because the time of God's coming into full fruition has come. We are at ground zero. The resurrection of God in these uncertain times is now. God, like faith, is now. This is why time is irrelevant to God. Because God is always on time. Like now! It's God's eternal, supreme, and authoritative right to inform us through the inspired and anointed messages of confessed sinners *born-again.* Saved by grace in the body of Christ Jesus, giving God the glory—*In the Moment!*

For I say, through the grace given to me, to everyone
who is among you, not to think of himself more highly
than he ought to think, but to think soberly, as God
has dealt to each one a measure of faith. For as we
have many members in one body, but all the members
do not have the same function, so we, being many, are
one body in Christ, and individually members of one
another. Having then gifts differing according to the
grace that is given to us, let us use them; if prophecy
let us prophesy in proportion to our faith; or ministry,
let us use it in our ministering; he who teaches, in
teaching; . . .

Romans 12:3-7

And this is what the lessons of life eternal is
about—getting it right. Not—be right, or my way or no
way! How will you know which way is which in the spirit
if you are not taught by the spirit. This must be done in
faith and be believed that this is the will of God. The spirit
within. The Holy Spirit one must be able to hear.

So then faith comes by hearing, and hearing by the
word of God.

Romans 10:17

Speaking of hearing, I heard something that really lets
me know why people don't know God personally. *Bottom*
line: They can't hear! Let me put it another way, for egos
are extremely fragile, defensive, and always in denial. Been

there, done that! The realization of hearing spiritually is, for many, lost. What we need here is an *attitude adjustment!* To me, it appears that most people aren't capable of listening because they are full of themselves, talking to themselves, congratulating themselves, or tearing themselves up. What a downer. To listen, one needs a submissive attitude, open to God! Seeking ye first the kingdom to the Holy Spirit and a willingness to act on what they hear. God does not talk to hear himself talk—*we do!* This is why Scriptures say:

> *Pride goes before destruction, and a haughty spirit before a fall.*
>
> Proverbs 16:18

Pride, a disdainful, haughty, self-indulgence. Biased on the side of an inflated ego. A real blockhead! The stumbling block that limits one to hear God clearly or to hear the Almighty God speaking through others to and for you. The anointed word. A God who only desires the best for you and from you. This is why I diligently and habitually keep my thoughts and mind open.

One morning, I was up writing, praying, and always conversing with God, my *Father* and dear friend, through the person of Christ Jesus, on the things God was preparing for me. God, through the mind of Christ—for I'm a sinner—not a blockhead! On this morning, in particular, my lesson was being prepared in my heart. The subject: Faith. My faith and the adherence to Paul's admonition to always have the full *armor of Christ* on and in place, each and every day. The wearing, watching as well as the praying. It was a preparation testing my readiness to thwart every trick and angle Satan might use to try my *patience*. To challenge my understanding of faith. My capability, by faith, to withstand Satan's bullshit on a daily basis as it lives amongst relatives, friends, neighbors, and all of society governed under the influence of Satan.

Unfortunately, God's children get lost. Lost in the inner sanctum of the spirit within the great stumbling block of **pride**, i.e., E-go, which edges God out. This is the hardest lesson for most. The eliminating of one's Ego—to let go and let God!

Christ Jesus took our sins to the cross, he bore the stripes for our illness and He redeemed us from Satan's grip. Freely did he do this, and freely he offers this to his children. Yet Satan does not give it up easily. He throws wrenches into the mix at every possible opportunity. Leading God's children into rebellion, denial, and dispute at every intersection.

Satan is the roaring lion of calamity and despair. Satan is Satan. A cosmic evil force that brings sorrow and distress. Satan's arsenal of weapons includes a retinue of ladies of the night: Miss Interpretation, Miss Information, Miss Communication, and Miss Take, Miss Fortune, Miss Meal. Then you end up driving = Miss Daisey.

These forces of darkness flee from the light of truth. God gives me a taste of this every day. The lesson of separation from his unbounded truth and light. When I turn my back on him, my world folds like a house of cards.

Prejudice, bias, violence, hate are dark and evil. They hasten death and shorten life. The light brings freedom; the dark brings bondage. Ya' dig? There is a difference.

When I experience these spiritual realizations, I realize the significance of why I must keep the full armor on. So I won't get penetrated by the daily cosmic fall out when the spirit of heaven and hell clash. All day long, in some form or another, no matter how minute it may appear to be, it can weaken your faith, and a mere flirtation with one of Satan's ladies can ignite spiritual strife. Yet when I make a conscious decision to wear my helmet of salvation, my breastplate of righteousness, my belt of truth, my shoes of peace, my shield of faith, and my Holy Bible as the Word of God in my heart and mouth, Satan has no way with me, nor will he have his way with you.

Failure to be prepared happens on a repetitive basis and, for many, is accepted as normal. The outcome: *Conflict!* Oh my God. And people really don't seem to know this is why we got **9/11**. This is why violence is domestic. It's da' human reality, politically. Correct? Satan's church and state approved, religiously sanction way of life—hell! And you really wonder why priests, pastors, rabbis, preachers, and ministers are adulterers, homosexuals, and child molesters. These whore mongers, liars, cut throat thieves are your world government—the *spirit of principality* ruling. And we help make it so—we! Da' people! It's the united way. Hello? See how God just let's me flow. You go, Mick E.

This is truly the blessing of freedom in America. The last place to freely express God. How to put church and state in check. A simple *attitude adjustment* about God's will for you in God's personal relationship in the body of Christ Jesus. To tell the truth, the whole truth, so God can help you and not yo' psychotic, dysfunctional, cultured, religious church and stated brainwashed, hypnotized, and cultivated E-go, has been conditioned to overreact or not act at all. Victims of Satan's www.dot.net. **Gotcha!** This includes yo' mama now! *In the Moment!* Ain't that a bitch!

It's our preconceived attitude about how things should go. Our emotions. Our thinking. Our will. Now the willful pride of a fallen world. This is why Jesus cried in the Garden of Gethsemane. It put *the fall* of pride in proper perspective. This bitter earth. Hate is ungodly. It tears the family of God up, yet God sacrificed his only begotten, and shit ain't spiritually improved. In fact, it's come full circle. USA, we are the world. Christ Jesus shed his blood for the world and then rose from the dead to affirm this gift. This bitter cup. It broke Jesus's heart. It caused *Our Father* to turn away from his only Son. For in that brief time, as Jesus hung on the cross, he bailed us out of hell and gave us eternal life. He redeemed us from the clutch of Satan's grip on the soul of man.

Because of what God has revealed to me, a believer in the body, I now have access to the mind of Christ. It's an understanding one receives. First, seek the Kingdom and all else will be added. God is good and doesn't lie. This is the enlightened reason for the believer to be living in the light of Christ. God's will being done!

This brings me to what I've been prepared to share in regards to all thus far said. This is a classroom. Not a rehearsal. *In the Moment!* where God is, and we must stay *In the Moment!* It can only be done according to his will. By our confession and personally witnessing for God, resisting the temptation to judge, hate, resent, curse, condemn, or bare false witness, you know character assassination, and still . . . still we all fall short. Especially a wretch like me! A confessed sinner! God still will use . . . me. Saved by grace good . . . gawd!

This leads me to the real point of my case and spiritual scenario *to lecture or not to lecture?* No! This is not the question. The question is: the answer to life! Life . . . it's a big classroom. A school of thought riddled with questions and answers, dos and don'ts that are reflected throughout our actions and behavior, whether responsible or irresponsible. Plus or minus, right or wrong, good or evil, and for some reason, we choose negatively, for the most part, in regards to God. We believe, but we don't trust. We go to church, but we do the ungodly. Why? We are the Church. Not the building. It's the way of the world. Always ass backward. You take Church to the building in order to fellowship—not congregate, stagnate, alienate, and procrastinate. That's the nature of the beast.

This is the equation of life and death. And the power of both are in your mouth. This is why we have to watch our thoughts. Because there's no telling what's gonna come outta yo' mouth. This is why this *life experience* is a classroom. The study of life and death. Feast or phantom.

Peace or war. A class action. The Son-day school of God. If you are a follower of Christ, the church is the perfect example of how to live in the world in peace and prosperity by using your faith as you were taught by the Holy Spirit within. How to discern and deal with confusion by those claiming to be in the body of Christ. A true confession. By your deeds and actions. By grace—the truth.

Now the church is being divided and conquered by the *Revisionists*. Taking the Word of God and revitalizing it with fictional historical data, nonevents, and dogma not authorized by the Holy Spirit of God Almighty. Institutionalized religious separation while degenerating from generation to degeneration. Why? They have lost their ability to listen and have become addicted to their own thoughts. Feelings have entered into the world of faith. Worldly feelings have no trust in God . . . only in what they perceive and feel. Plain and simple—they don't trust God! Why? Because they don't know the truth. For them. There is no right answer.

And it will always be the same when you hear God. You hear true love. The truth of love that sets you free to forgive, reconcile, fix, heal, grow, and know you know God. Mainly because you obeyed and did something lovable for God toward another for the love of God. Even the enemy! The Great Commission is to love the Lord your God with all your heart, mind, spirit, and strength, and the second commandment is like unto it: Love your neighbor as yourself. And who is your neighbor? Everybody!

This love of God is so simple and apropos to the lesson of life. It's private tutoring, attending the private classroom of Christ all in the mind. It's so beautiful. Just shut your eyes, sit still, and listen and know. For this is how faith comes by hearing. Hearing by the Word of the Lord. Yet! Faith without good works is dead. Good works according to God's will. This is a lesson the true believer must know and remember and always do *In the Moment!* Your faith is tested and tempted to do the ungodly and not God's true will, which is love. Which brings me to the heart of the subject, the lesson of the moment. Titled: Can you hear the bullshit of Satan? Or, do you really think it's God or *God's will be ours?*

It's all about the will. Our will or God's will. Which *WILL* will we listen to and obey and follow? Since we all fall short of the glory of God. We all have the stumbling block of E-go—even the Elect. This is the spiritual flaw Satan plays on—our E-go. This is where Satan's temptations entice us all. For all fall short—even the elect. And the temptations are so smooth—cloud nine—still the world of Satan, *a ball of confusion!*

Therefore, as believers we must surrender to the right of way—God's way! There are no compromises. If you choose to follow God's will, your will becomes submissive to his. And when you abandon your will for God's will, you win!

> If anyone desires to come after me, let him deny
> himself, and take up his cross, and follow me. For

whoever desires to save his life will lose it, but
whoever loses his life for my sake will find it.

Matthew 16:24-25

It's your call, your free will, you make the choice. It's an object lesson—a daily test you are called upon in order to secure your faith. This is the **Faith Walk**. The objective of heaven here on earth. Free will. It's your inalienable rights.

This calling upon your faith can happen anytime, any place, and everywhere. One of my numerous calls was one I remember in particular. And one of my most cherished "clashes" for God where I stepped out to take the *hit* and be like Christ and except the next nail. It's the cross-check! *The Passion of Christ*. Hamma Time!

I was nailed with Christ Jesus for the zillionth time on March 17, 2002—St. Patrick's Day. Shamrocked and shellacked. I guess I got the *luck of the Irish*. So keep those nails a'com'n! *Praise God!* Nail on, brother, and by the way, where's my cross? Here I was at 5:00 AM in da' moan'n! I say *moan'n* 'cause as beautiful as this would turn out in the end, it was another example of faith teaching love. For me, I would still know it's moan'n'. *This is the callin'* as referred to in 1 Peter 2:21.

It was the way the clash began and had to go to support the lesson to be taught. This is the catch: You've got to live it and feel the sting of the pain of conflict, and the spirit within will give you the comprehensive spiritual understanding afterward. The revelation of *good moan'n'*. The healing of forgiveness and the trying of yo' faith. Okay, let's not forget that it's 5:00 AM in the *moan'n'*. The phone rings. I'm sitting at my dinner table, writing, praying, conversing, and laughing **In the Moment** with the joy of knowing God knows what's up, why it's up, and what is about to go down. This is the all-knowing God I'm hanging out with. The good morning continues to shine as the phone continues to ring. I answer and am lit up by the light and power of God's love, "Good morn'n, Mick E. Jones at your service." Then I hear this really uplifting, lilting voice, saying, "How you doing?"

The voice was cheerful and buoyant. It had a rich comic feel to the light baritone texture with the coloration of a second tenor tone. Not quite an Irish tenor. More like a flatlander, *the salt of the earth*—Bluegrass. The Jimmy Dean, John Denver West Virginia flavor—a good ole boy sound. "How's it going? I just thought I'd call to see how everything is going. What are you up to? I was talking with my mama, so I decided to give you a call." Now all this is good. It really sounds so sincere. The only problem is I don't have a clue as to who it is.

"Things are going great. God is good. Now . . . who am I talking to?" We laughed, then the caller said, "Uncle Mick E. It's me . . . Kenny."

I'm literally taken aback. "Kenny . . . who?"

"Your nephew! Kenny Biter."

Now I am really taken back . . . and back and back. My mouth hangs open, as I come to myself, saying, "Kenny Biter! Watcha doin' callin' me at 5:00 AM?" I laughed as I said it.

Kenny protested mildly, No! It's eight o'clock, Uncle Mick E.!" I was very amused. In fact, I was laughing when I said, "Kenny, you're just like your mama. You look at the clock, and the clock reads eight o'clock. Then your mind says call Mick E., and you are correct, it's eight o'clock there. It's five o'clock here. California."

Kenny was very apologetic, and I could hear that he was genuinely embarrassed. He began to sound hurt and distressed to the point of sounding anguished. "Uncle Mick E., I'm sorry. I didn't realize it was that early."

I could hear the sorrow in his voice. My spirit received his sincere regret. He thought he'd caused me some discomfort or inconvenience and couldn't seem to find the right words to fix it.

I tried to pull the situation back into the upbeat groove we had when he first called. "Kenny, don't sweat it. I was up. I've been up. Up and kick'n it with the Lord. We were just talk'n about situations that come up seemingly inconveniently. With the understanding of the Lord—it's cool. But! Don't forget to check the clock—eight your time, five in California. You just like yo' mama." I was really enjoying this. I mean, who cares what time it is? My nephew, Kenny Biter, was calling. This is a blessing. "Uncle Mick E.," he said, "I'm sorry. I know I should have known better." I laughed, saying, "It's okay. Just be better at check'n the clock. 8:00 AM yo' time is 5:00 AM my time."

"Uncle Mick E., I said *I'm sorry!* I know how to tell time. I just didn't realize or think of the time difference. I'm sorry. So you don't have to tell me how to tell time. Okay?"

I suddenly heard and felt the tension mount. It seemed our joyous, uplifting lilt had come down to what was being perceived as *corrective*. It was obvious Kenny received and somehow misunderstood my words and statements as *corrective* or a reprimand. Perhaps even judgment. "Oh my God, Kenny!" I slowly began, deliberately taking my time because I know I have a *motor mouth*; and if your hearing ain't in tune, or you're trying to tune me out, I'm slaughter on Fifth Avenue to your ears. And your mind will snap. Yes! You *will* get an attitude! Thus, the heart of the lesson.

"Kenny, let me say this as slowly and as clearly as possible. Eight o'clock, five o'clock or tickety tock, you didn't wake me up. Even if you had, I don't care. I'm up kicking it with the Lord who has prepared me for these moments. For you. Who cares about the o'clock. It's time you and I are able to talk." I thought this would be the clincher . . . wrong!

"Uncle Mick E., I just called to talk. I don't need to be lectured to." Almost whispering, I say compassionately, "My intentions, Kenny, aren't to lecture, period. Can you hear me? It ain't about us. It's about God in us. God wanting us to be family." That went over like a lead balloon. Kenny went to wherever he goes.

Then . . . *snap*! He snapped and began yelling, "Uncle Mick E.! I don't need a lecture, and I don't want you lecturing me. I don't need to be lectured to!" And he abruptly hung up! I'll be damned!

I stood there, with the cordless phone in my hand, the antenna against my closed mouth. I began to tap it against my nose. I could feel a tear slowly rolling down my face, then another and another, and I prayed softly for forgiveness. I got up from the table and walked over to the family desk. I looked in the lower drawer, got out a card, and returned to the table. I sat down and began to write a letter of apology and regret about the incident that had just occurred. I was saddened rather than hurt. It wasn't about hurt—that's for egos and the flesh. This was a matter of the spirit and the heart of a young man who tried to reach out to the unlikely. This was a need. Not a desire. It was a *spiritual litmus test.* Always a lesson for us all. It's always about the good of the whole. The unity, the one accord of God's love. To be reconciled.

> *Now then, we are ambassadors for Christ, as though God were pleading through us; we implore you on Christ's behalf, be reconciled to God.*
>
> 2 Corinthians 5:20

Reconciliation! What a natural symbol of what Jesus died for and why Christ Jesus was resurrected to restore to God the family of man. This included Kenny and myself. To be restored in and adopted as sons of God. This is the enlightened reasoning. The substance of the subject and the object of the lesson. How faith works. That God is—real!

Now here's a real twist in the reconciliation of God's family through faith in Christ Jesus. Kenny's sister, Amy, was in Hollywood. She'd been here a couple of days. Amy and I had, not long before, worked through this very same lesson. It was a different class, but the same principle. Naturally, the same results God's will being done. God always wins. God reaps what God sows.

Anyway, I related the phone incident to Amy. She had come by to take her Aunt to dinner. After she heard the story, she laughed, remarking, "That's Kenny. When Kenny does that to me, I say, 'Whatever.'" We both laughed. *Whatever,* still it's God's family reconciled. The laughter felt familiar, like family. Family matters to God, *Our Father!*

Standing in the doorway, watching Amy and Sue get into Amy's luxury rent-a-car, I couldn't help but reflect for a moment that Amy was here to hob-knob with some of Hollywood's elite—the rich and famous. She was here raising funds for Emerson College, and she's very good at it. She has her mother's social grace and determination.

Closing the door, I immediately started having memory flash backs. Back to when I first met Kenny Biter. He was with his mother, Noelle Sullivan, also known as Carole Biter. She had four children. Kenny, his sister Kathleen, brother David, and Amy. All young and very well behaved. And all very lovable. Especially Kenny! He had loving eyes and blushed when he looked at me. The kind of blush when a child's spirit chooses from the heart a stranger to love. A child's instinct goes to love. The precious part of a child's spirit is to trust in the pureness of its feelings. Kenny had that look. And a smile to match. He was so adorable.

His mother, Carole Noelle, was the center of the conversation, talking about her childhood and her reflections of their family—the Sullivans. The conversation usually stayed close to the Sullivans.

Carole Noelle is my wife's sister. When Sue and I were newlyweds, Carole made it a point to check on us. She seemed to be the family historian. Because she had the *411* on everybody. She also seemed to be the family chairperson. The CEO—*da' ruler.*

Listening to Carole Noelle, I began to look more closely at the kids. This is when I would see Kenny just beaming. He would be staring at me with a big smile, talking through his eyes. Eventually, the kids would all commence touching me. They were using wrestling and little tag gestures to communicate their feelings. It was Kenny, more than the others, who appeared to hug more than wrestle. He would hold on to my arm, caressing and actually comparing our skin. His white skin next to my summer tanned dark brown skin was a delightful contrast for him. He was comfortable with it all. It was no big deal. He'd decided, at least the way I read it, that this was not an issue. That was a moment of innocence. In the school of life, issues and lessons are learned in the process innocence fades. We all fall! *Bombs away!*

This first encounter of the heart I had with Kenny was, ironically enough, in Boston, Massachusetts. where the first American patriot was killed—a *black* man by the name of **Mr. Crispus Attucks** *(circa 1770)*.

The next encounter would be in Allentown, New Jersey, if memory serves me correctly. It was a feeling of *Guess Who Came to Dinner.* I was being scrutinized.

Nothing offensive, just polite observation. It was as if I were a *science project*—an experiment that had already been conceived, tried, and proven, then categorized. It's now *status quo*. Clinically modified behavior with premeditated verbal responses. These were the vibes I felt from the adult members who made up the various branches of our connected family. Bio and extended. I'd been stamped Approved and passed by the family board members, who were usually Sullivans. Who became Biters, who became Sullivans! Sullivan—Sullivans. Sullivans who became Houses. *The House of Sullivan.* Usually, you ended up in a Sullivan house. It's all good.

It was an interesting time for me, packed with fond memories. The greatest of which was seeing Kenny crawling around on the floor. He would slither along behind the couch, then look over the top, unnoticed by the adults who were too busy scrutinizing and drinking. But! Leave it to Kenny. He would find a way to see me, to touch me. Playfully walking through the living room, he'd manage to somehow touch my Afro. These were the fabulous seventies! Politically correct, government approved, integration (though not necessarily a united nation). It was a psychedelic facade of "we are family, peace and love." Yeah right!

The love Kenny had for me as a child shifted with the coming of age and Sullivan isolationism. The natural instinct of love got whitewashed, narrowed to tunnel vision with loss of hearing—separate and unequaled. The placing of loyalty to the flesh instead of the spirit of God. The gift of love lost and now riddled with hang-ups.

Lost *In the Moment,* perhaps . . . lost forever? I doubt it. For this is the purpose of Son-day school—the lesson, the course, and intention of Christ to bring together that which was lost.

> *For the son of man has come to save that which was lost.*
> Matthew 18:11

And I will not lose Kenny. I confess this before the class, which is translated in spirit, through the Scriptures, inspired by God, as *confession is good for the soul.* I confess Christ before witnesses of believers and nonbelievers, he's *my personal Savior,* to whom I'm commissioned to be a part of the reconciliation of mankind. So, in the spirit and body of Christ, I reach out to my darling nephew, Mr. Ken Biter, whom I have loved from the very day I saw him as a child. Before he was conformed by the world. God, *Our Father,* in all his wisdom, revealing the core of a good man, whom God had prepared for me on March 17, 2002, St. Patrick's Day, at 5:30 AM. I was ready. Because when you call a child of God in the body of Christ, God *Our Father* responds, and God will always let you know he heard you. This is the hearing by faith—a spiritual law.

It Is Written. This is the purpose of *Son-day school.* To teach and reveal the truth, and the truth shall make you free from the hang-ups of the world. This lecture is now complete, and class is dismissed.

God Bless Y'all, America the Beautiful!

U-Never Really Know
What . . . I Mean

Hey, Rich! Yeah! You're rich and wealthy in so many, many ways. If you would only see yourself the way God let's me see you, you're something to behold! Spiritual gold. A precious soul. Richard da' Lionhearted. Alice 'n Wonderland. A Wizard of Odds and Ends.

I bet this is a sir-prize, *yassur*! I hope a pleasant and spiritually appreciated surprise. If not, I must admit, it's still April, so maybe it's a fool's thang. That would conceivably make me an April fool!

Ahh! That's so beautiful—a fool's metaphor. No foolin'! I speak as a fool. Not in jest, for I will never trifle. I am a fool 4-U! All joking aside, it's a good thing, for it brings the April showers and May flowers. A bouquet of life. The truth be known: You are loved! How you like me now?

Life is soo very interesting, right? You never really know life, do you? Does anyone? For instance, you never know who's going to really B-4 you in life, do you? As individual participants in the Life, we're all guilty of thinking it's ours! Gotcha, April fools!

I have known you, or have known of you, since 1971. If senility has not affected my recall, we are talkin' forty-two years. In the sphere of family association and all things considered, that's a lot of years of quality family time. The association, in family time terms, was mainly through hearsay. You'd hear them say something 'bout me, and I'd hear them say something 'bout you. Now we're talkin' 'bout how shit happens! It's a factor in family associations. Conflict is a human dilemma. A family reunion can set the stage for conflict. However, through all the many reunions, you and I have only been in the same place together, perhaps six times—give or take. Sort of similar to the way Michael Jackson and Diana Ross used to be.

When Sue and I married, it was only the second time I'd seen you. But what comes to mind is the reception where I distinctly remember how you appeared. Your aura was heavy, dank, and clouded. You had a trapped look about you. Like a hostage. Like a puppet on a string. *Zing!* went the strings of my heart. Like Jesus—nailed! Stuck! I absorbed all that pain. The Passion of Christ. I felt your pain. I mean you seemed torn between two worlds—the one you were in, and the one you wanted to be in. And you were up to your eyeballs with it! Period! Enough is enough! Sadly, I saw it in your eyes, especially as the evening wore on. Drinking has a way of unraveling emotional hairballs and allowing the hidden and dark side to spill out. The lost and the trapped. Yeah! That's how I read you—lost, trapped, and suppressed. J. Michael has the same look! It's not misery . . . it's the void. You both are *floaters* out there in the abyss.

That's the way you looked at our wedding reception. Lost. Then, as if a curse or blessing had gone astray, you miraculously morphed into *the Clump* when a cluster of family members (in-laws), who, like you—and to this day—regard me as a family associate. A paradoxical oxymoron. My people. My family in-laws. Carol Biter/Noelle (still a Carol) Sullivan, Rube Biter/Rob Sullivan, and J. Michael Sullivan. Naturally, there was Fran, Nathaniel, and Rebecca—*the Houses*. The family crew of which you're the husband and father.

You all were there! At **our** wedding. Clumped together—*the Clumpsters*. A traveling family circuit court. The *N'Laws*, who appointed themselves to high-ranking officials of life 4-life. Judges and prosecuting attorneys. The family *DAs* as well as the jury. The Looky Lous. Baby Boomers. Kennedy Lovers. The Beatles, John Denver, and Barbra *Streisand* worshipers. Frank Sinatra, His Royal Majesty *Ol' Blue Eyes*.

The Clumpsters were adorable, funny and a joy, like the Keystone Cops on an outing. You gotta love *the Clumpsters*. All of this becomes clearer and clearer the more I think about our marriage. I'm sitting here in a contemplative mood, recalling and notating passed events ala men-a-*pause*. I begin to put daily stuff on hold as I really start to concentrate, focusing ***In the Moment!*** Telepathically, I travel back in time as an *overviewer!* The one who sees over. In order to get an in-depth perspective on the understanding gained through this method of observation, seeing through to the light at the end of the tunnel, I begin to generate an out-of-body/out-of-mind experience. A therapeutic spiritual event. To better crystallize and gain the truth; a spiritual insight, a ritual to myself as a living testament. Sharing the lesson of the experience in and on the journey . . . the journey of life. I'm blessed to have the capability to articulate and express what I witness. The experience of living in the *truth*. **It is written . . .**

I'm beginning to remember, with vivid clarity, how you looked as one of *the Clumpsters*. Clustered together yet divided like you were not there—long division yet a close ass-sumption. You seemed to embody the lyrics of *the O'Jay's* song, "Your body's here with me. But your mind is on the other side of town." This was the way you looked in the midst of *the Clumpsters*, standing, holding your baby son, Nathaniel, "Nate da' Great," who'd grabbed the spotlight from Rebecca of *Sunnybrook*, your daughter. Your firstborn—Daddy's little girl! Center of attention with cheeks like Apple Annie but, without warning, had been reduced to second banana. To a *boy*, nonetheless! Nuts over the banana split!

She stood clinging on to your pants leg. She had a dazed look. Her little girl spirit knew what her mind couldn't conceive and heart couldn't receive—sex discrimination! Separate but never equal. Sibling stress. The man/woman relationship. Childhood/adult stumbling block. An adult suppressed psychic mess, and looking at you both, you each had the same emotional demeanor. It's what your face and body language expressed.

Rebecca was carrying the weight of childhood—sibling stress. And you . . . Don Quixote, *the man of La Mancha*, looked very put upon. The burden of being a father and a husband had you compressed, depressed, and pissed, but in a quiet way. Dare I say "**sad**"? You didn't look centered or glad. Ah, here it is . . . *abandoned*. Richard *Abandoned* House. And *a house is not a home, if there's no one living there*. Huh, homie? Get my drift? House 4-Sale in a depressed market. It's not lookin' good.

Then there was New York. The city that never goes to sleep. I guess this explains why everyone's irritable and edgy. Got to have some sleep, yet it was *Sleepless in New York*, which became the setting for our initial meeting. This was long before the wedding. We endured a cold reception, which became the basis of our formal introduction. The New York City the **BIG CHILL** was present in your humble abode . . . be it ever so humble. There's no place like home!

That's very true if you live in Kansas . . . Dorothy! But dis here's New Yawk City . . . the home of some of the most notorious mayors in American history, like La Guardia, Lindsay, Dinkins, to name a few. Cold! *Brrr.*

These above-mentioned political heads of NYC would pale in comparison to my facing *the tribunal family court* of NYC. Court was in session the moment I stepped into your humble abode, which also functioned as the center of the family judicial system's *home court rules*. Listening with my inner ear, I could hear the phrase, "Order in the court . . . 'cause here comes the judge. All rise!"

All I could say was, "What's goin' on? Waz up?" Slowly, I glanced around the room. It seemed familiar. I've been to court before! But never before the Royal Court of NYC! Suddenly, I'm standing before Her Majesty *Queen Mother* Peggy Sullivan. Ah, tis the luck of the Irish!

Although you were on the jury, you nevertheless appeared absent. Somehow you had become *foreman by proxy*. Your body was in, but your mind was out. Well, you know the song. My point being, like most people on jury duty, you were there because you couldn't get out of it. The real deal. The judge was yo' wife's mama! You silently and diplomatically served as a very quiet conscientious objector who dutifully dispensed true patriotism as family politics required. *Da' Bush-shit!*

At the tribunal, I was interrogated and closely scrutinized. However, I was *acquitted*. I got my family green card and am now a *legal alien ass-sociate family member* in reasonably good standing with all. Okay . . . a few. All right, ONE! Sue, my wife. Ain't life grand? You feel me? I know . . . **U-Never Really Know What . . .** *I Mean!*

The more I got to know the many members of the family ass-sociation, and their descendants, and their kids *(literally, the offsprings)*, the more valid became the old cliché: "The apple doesn't fall far from the tree." So true, and the proof rested in *the Clumpsters*

The baby Clumpsters were identical to their elders. They got me! Here I am family, and this is family business—a tradition—a cultural thang. It plays out, in principle, like *The Sopranos* . . . if you're black somebody gonna pull a gun on you! So the deal is this: *Don't take yo' gun to town, Bill.* Leave yo' gun at home, son. That was the theme at the heart of my *gun experience*, which would take place during my first visit to Swarthmore, Pennsylvania.

You guys hadn't been out of New York long, maybe three or four years, at most. Anyway, Nathaniel, your darling son, and my nephew pulled a gun on me. He was about five at the time. This *gun-frontation* happened during one of those awkward moments we were having when we were having a conversation, which was unfortunately starting to deteriorate badly. A monologue was developing in response to a misinterpretation of polite social conversation. You know how it goes—*nice to nasty.* Conversation laced with suppressed anger, coloring the subtext with hidden intents revealing the true feelings hidden beneath the polite banter. Sort of talking one way while walking the other way.

For instance, as the host, you might have been thinking, *I wish you weren't here, and if you would be so kind and ever so gracious, would you dignify us all and please leave . . . depart! Like now! If not sooner . . . bye!* **Bravo!**

Alas, you did not and because you suppressed the truth, you drank just a little bit more. What about the naive guest—the April fool? His response to the suppressed vibes seething beneath the surface? They were felt and seen in the eyes and heard in the tonal inflections of the voice. The vessel of the suppression clearly seen on the host's face. Your face—a portrait photographed in my mind with perfect clarity became a classic *picture worth a thousand words. The fool* a.k.a. *the guest* understood perfectly.

This moment was a moment of revelation and contradiction. I thought, *Jesus Christ, my host can't stand my guts. My host hates me. Why am I here? Then again, why not! God is good. So this is all good!* And I lifted my glass and drank!

This was the kind of vibe we were in . . . then and now. It's the norm, for the most part. The normal undertone of suppression that represents the true intent of *the Clumpster Clustered Clan.* A child, who is my nephew and your darling son, was the only one truthful enough **In the Moment** to recognize my visit for what it truly was then and is now. Tart and edgy.

Even in his infancy, Nathaniel "Nate da' Great" demonstrated a certain inherited mental insight and a natural instinct that allowed him to act **In the Moment** with innocent precision, charging me with **Disorderly Conduct** by a family green card *legal alien ass-sociate family member.* Who's out of order? Court is in session. *Bang!* This was official! After all, this was his *"daddy's"* House, and he was **a House!** Clearly, I was under **House arrest.**

If my memory serves me correctly—politically, that is—then it will do this next segment justice. For it was at this juncture, Nathaniel said, "You're under arrest. Stop talking. You're going to jail!" I was speechless! I wasn't saying nothing with my mouth. In my mind, I thought, *I'm going to jail? No $200 . . . even if I pass GO? What about a GET-OUT-OF-JAIL-FREE card?* While those thoughts gathered more and more momentum, I stood waiting on **Nate da' Great** to say som'em, but he remained tight-lipped and lockjawed.

There I stood, like a man about to hang, with the noose blowin' in the breeze, and I'm like what . . . *What? I think this is getting tight! I need some help!* I look to the jury, appealing to them. I look at you. Then to Fran . . . at Sue! And finally at Rebecca, who was clinging to you in an effort not to loose you in the family court system.

Shaking my head at last, I begin to come to grips with the grim reality of the moment: *I'm going to jail!* My First Amendment rights had just vanished. *KA-BOOM!* Up in smoke, and all that remained was my right to silence! That's as good as it got! No reading of my Miranda rights, no showing of any official papers, no warrant—no nothing! No attorney and no phone call! Just, "You have the right to remain quiet, silent, shad up . . . these are the HOUSE RULES."

Turning back around, I looked sympathetically at the arresting officer, giving him my *sad sack look*. I hung my head, furrowed my brow, and looked at him with my *faithful hound dog eyes* . . . all—all to no avail. Nathaniel stood unmoved. Sort of like Wyatt Earp at the O.K. Corral. He had that "I ain't moved/no sympathy" look. I saw it so clearly in his cold, beady little baby eyes. His little infant face scrunched up with nostrils flared. He was all business! HE WAS, after all, the **Sheriff!** He was the arresting officer and had his cowboy suit and boots on. His cowboy hat cocked to one side, a slick neck scarf, but most importantly, he wore **the badge,** and it read **Sheriff**. He had a gun, which was drawn and cocked. You know, *In the Moment* the thought occurred to me, *This ain't no joke, and it's a good thing this isn't Columbine 'cause what's that old saying,* "Out of the mouths of babes . . ." *Well, what about dere hands? The one wit' da' gun?*

That bit of wisdom confirmed in my mind a bold fact: **Children today ain't right!** Something is spiritually wrong with them. They're off-center. Let's not forget . . . Hitler was once a baby too! An ugly baby, perhaps, but a baby nonetheless! Bush, very serious birth defect. But still a baby.

This is why history repeats itself. You can be dysfunctional and still be the head of state. Hail to the chief. History reproduced in the genes. The DNA—sick!

Little things mean a lot, especially since you and I have never really gotten to know one another. What little exchange that has occurred had significant impact. No matter how lightly it may have appeared to have come across, there was always a heavy social undercurrent.

Take the time you came to our 1209 Boylston Street apartment in Boston. It was no tea party. Nor was it a *Remember* battle of the Alamo scenario. I don't recall the occasion or circumstances that brought you to Boston. However, you were a welcomed visitor in Myspace. Yo' space. You were family, not an ass-sociate. This wasn't the masters. No green card or jacket was necessary. This is real America. Our Pledge of Allegiance to a God who **can be trusted!** *Our Father.* He is not a respecter of persons. True love is like that. Welcome to God's world!

You joined other family members in the living room. Everyone was seated around the wooden picnic dining table. Gathered in the round was brother Pat Allen, who was closing in on his PhD in psychology from Harvard. Sister Deborah "Big Deb" Jennings who was an assistant administrative consultant at an adult home for the mentally challenged. My precious Sue—my gift and my wife—a true blessing! And naturally, there was me, who was honing and perfecting **Mick E.'s Lounge Act.**

As you settled into the family circle, Sue said, "Are you hungry?" Your response was, "What do you have?" Sue beamed and said, "Smothered chicken, greens, etc." With one of your classic deadpan expressions, undercut with the driest of humor, and smothered in a vibe of suppressed sarcasm, you shrugged your shoulders in a self-amusing chuckle, saying, "That's typical."

The candlelight wine, and dinner went smoothly. The air was cordial, polite, frivolously warm, and sincere. Filled with unpretentious conversation. Good chatter. Never becoming heavy, burdensome, or profound. Simply congenial and hospitable. No church and state, no politics—incorrect or correct—no, it felt like idealism. How ideal! The art of being a human family. Quite unlike my personal experiences amongst *the Clumpsters.*

Here at *1209 America* you weren't interrogated or attacked. No trial, no arrest, or no threats of going to jail. No judgments. There were no violations of your First Amendment rights. This was Martin Luther King's "I Have a Dream." No green card or civil rights necessary. This was the real America, complete with character and contents of the family—goodwill. We were all just getting along, and God's will was being done.

As Sue was clearing the table, I suggested that we play some cards while Barbra Streisand was singing in the background, "People who need people are the luckiest people in the world." As you see, this was a defining moment in **our** American family.

Going over to the bookshelf, I got a pack of cards; and as I took out the cards, you were sipping your wine watching me like a riverboat gambler who has seen many a slick card dealer. As I began shuffling the cards, you requested like a professional player, "What's the game?" Downing your wine, you waited for my response with a great poker face. I smiled as I placed the cards on the table and replied, "Spades." I sounded like Barry White. You could feel the theme from *Shaft*. You seemed to softly grind your teeth as I watched your jaw muscles flexing. *Spades!* With a Clint Eastwood glint in your eye, you seemed to almost whisper, "Make my day!"

You could feel the theme music from *The Good, Bad and Ugly* roll across the room. You shook your head, squinted your misty blue eyes, and exhaled. A faint smile dawned when you said, "That figures!" You really looked at home, homey! Like one of the boys, you belonged. It was a good evening. Family is like that.

There are many things that make the human experience so delicate and fragile. However, I believe *belonging* is the most powerful experience one can have. So unique God had to experience it and reaffirm that the human experience is worth saving for his created self, who is neither male nor female.

Then there was the redeeming Passion of Christ moment. The grace filled moment of truly understanding *the Clumpsters*. That awareness came with my green card when I went back to another in-law reunion at Allentown, New Jersey, where the major players, the family board of directors, were present: The Biters, Houses, Sullivans, Heffernans, and the astonishing Strikers had all gathered for another family barbeque and drink fest. Bottoms up! Alcoholic Anonymous. *Note:* the alcoholic is always the last to know.

This all had an urban cowboy feel to it. Actually, the feel came more from your Western motif. Just a hint of *Bluegrass* and a *Brokeback Mountain* allure. A new sheriff in town. *Howdy, partnah! Ya-hoo. Y'all sa, y'all sa . . . Billy Buck, Buck!*

I'm half-humming, "I'm an old cowhand from the Rio Grande . . ." I circulated through all the adults, children, and grandchildren. Oddly enough, though, there were no grandparents present at the roundup! As I circled through the hacienda—the Ponderosa—I could've sworn I saw *Hoss* and *L'il Joe*! I exaggerate some, but for real, the Biter's Allentown house was spacious. Plenty of yard space, both front and back. Rube and Carol had it going on. Rube turned me on to John Denver. My props . . . Brother Ass-sociate Rube, you really are beautiful. Love ya', man! See! I *am* man enough!

To get an idea of how I felt you had to walk, or float along, in my shoes. First, I had grapple with why I was there. I was like the Invisible Man. Every once in a while I was actually recognized. Deja vu! It was quite startling—like I was dreaming. But I wasn't asleep. It was if I were in a trance, and somebody would say, "Oh, there you are," or "Having a good time?" With glazed over eyes, they would flash a bright smile as if a charitable work had just been done. It was like an LSD trip. It was surreal. The truth . . . *what it wuz* . . . **iz** *what it wuz! So be it! Good gawd! Hit me, James Brown!*

As I slipped in and out of anonymity, I ventured into the backyard to hang out with the only other family ass-sociate, who cared about me outside of Sue, my ever so darling and precious wife, who I absolutely adore, and that was Daisy. A big, huge, and very lovable St. Bernard. She was caged in a spacious pen with plenty of room to run around, but not to run free! It was easy to see through Daisy's eyes that she was a free spirit. I went into the cage. She seemed so happy to see me! Even though this was our first *rendezvous*, she seemed extremely happy to see me. We were of the same kindred universal spirit. Love.

She jumped up on me almost as if she were trying to hug me. Like a woman. She was licking me like a crazed woman, whose clock was running at a fever pitch. And as things intensified, it appeared that Cinderella would turn into a pumpkin if she didn't beat the clock. Timing was everything for Daisy, and it was time out for me. Anyone have a towel?

Later, I learned why Daisy was so crazed. She was in heat! Really, a **hot dog!** *Wuff . . . wuff.* In spite of that, I may have some animal charisma. I know I got some "wuff wuff" in me. Daisy done made me sure of that. She tuned me in!

Going from the *hot love* of Daisy, I reentered my invisible ass-sociate state, complete with invisible benefits. Since no one noticed me, I was able to see and hear things that would Jerry Curl my Afro in seconds flat. Among other things, I overheard one of the ass-sociate family members taking a hard line toward me. The reality of what I was hearing stopped me in my tracks! One member said to the other, "If you ever bring him to our home, I'll divorce you!" I thought, *What a man!* I went right back out to Daisy and got me another kiss. *Wuff . . . wuff . . .*

While I was hanging out with Ms. Daisy, I got to thinking about what I'd just heard. It brought to mind an old story my blind uncle, Uncle Jim James Allen—the Mighty Elephant—told me one day.

The gist of the story goes like this:

> *There was a man. This old white man, who hated the Negro—colored people. The old white man was in charge of a predominately Negro labor task force. [We talkin' Teddy Roosevelt times. I don't know. It could've been Franklin Delano. Anyway . . .] The old white man would always boast to the mainly Negro task force, who he usually referred to as "niggas" and would proudly boast, while patting his*

bull dog on the head, "I'd rather be a dead dog than be a live nigga!" He'd laugh then sic his bulldog on a colored man, yelling, "Get that, nigga!" The dog would proceed to attack.

Well, this one particular day, the dog proceeded to attack the colored man, and the man ran into traffic . . . nearly getting hit. He somehow, miraculously, averted a car. The bulldog wasn't so fortunate. He got hit. **Bam!** *Killed instantly [awe]. A crowd gathered and watched while the white man hysterically mourned the loss of his dog, who was his friend and his family. Feeling the owner's pain, the man of color offered his condolences. He said, "Sorry 'bout yo' dog, boss. There he is [shaking his head] a dead dog . . . and I'm alive . . . nigga [pause] no offense, boss."*

Here is another situation that puts us in the same place and space—**Steak and Brew.** Remember that? Your old stomping grounds? Your place of employment during the wonderful '70s? You were the manager of the Steak and Brew. You were **the man!**

Correct me if I'm wrong, sometimes my mind plays tricks on me. If this is not a mental trick *(the mind is a trick-E place to live)*, I was upstairs. I believe I was on the fifth floor in one of the business offices over the restaurant. I was attending what turned out to be a big time media event for ABC. I was invited to this occasion by my brother, Gene Clark, and his company. They were doing a screening of what I perceived as a sort of preemptive propaganda piece for America's early involvement in the Middle East crisis, even though we were still very much stuck in *Trickie Dickie's* Vietnam excursion. To me, this presentation was like a Coming Attraction. A trailer at the theater to promote the next world disaster. Produced, directed, and commercially sold—it's big business! Crisis marketing, preeminent domain, masters of the universe, fear fondling for the voyeuristic. A spiritual vice—war. The anti Christ of *Thou Shall Not Kill.*

The preeminent event was being screened and critiqued before a private viewing. The critics were a blend of international members of the Un-united Nations, state officials and important media types and figureheads.

I began mixing and mingling, moving and grooving, chatting and listening, eating and drinking all types of elegantly prepared and delicious foods and drinks. In the midst of all this official pomp and gluttony, I was able to get some interesting verbal foreign exchanges to think about and speak on. I used the Da Vinci Code style. To make it up as I go.

After all, I'd downed a couple of glasses of Veuve Clicquot Ponsardin, so I was internationally mellow, enjoying the foreign verbal exchange. It was unreal—politically correct yet making absolutely no sense.

As I sauntered and glided glowingly through the room (sliding like Fred Astaire—I was way to *glowy* to do the Nicholas Brothers, which is neither here nor there—I had social moves with an international flair), one dignified gentleman stopped me with a very engaging yet inquisitive glare. He wore a turban, a thick mustache that continued down into his beard. He was dressed in a tan cotton summer suit with brown shirt and a yellow bow tie. He had a brown polka dot pocket square with some sort of medallion or pin on the pocket, and his shoes, they were brown and white Oxford saddle locks.

He appeared to be from somewhere in the Mediterranean. He looked and sounded like a character out of *Casablanca*. He asked me three questions. He fired them off one right after the other. "Why are you here?" "Where are you from?" "Who are you?" Then it was like we were placed on pause. We stood frozen in a live freeze frame. Mannequins . . . a set of international dummies. The dummying up was broken when a passing waiter asked, "Hors d'oeuvre?" He was offering something stuck on a stick.

I was uncertain if we were going to exchange names or not. So until I learned who this suave, olive-skinned butterfly was, I will call him Mr. Turban. In any event, he was now joyously chewing as he asked, "You were saying?" He looked at me with great expectation, as if he was about to hear a profound revelation. Befuddled and amused, I began to cough, clutching my left hand to my mouth. I chuckled, thinking to myself, it was like being an enigma wrapped in a riddle. My cough eased, and I found myself saying absolutely nothing. I couldn't help but think, *Absurdity versus diplomacy, this is getting ticklish!* Thoughtfully distracted, Mr. Turban began stroking his beard between his thumb and forefingers, then rubbing his chin provocatively by pulling on his bottom lip. It was a masterful execution. Refocused, he once again expressed his concerns, "Who are you? Why are you here? And where are you from?"

In the midst of this, someone announced that we should now take our seats. The movie was ready to be reviewed. Thus, we were addressed: "Ladies and gentlemen, sit back and relax. We hope you enjoy it. Following immediately after, we would appreciate your candid remarks, your likes and dislikes." We started toward our seats. Mr. Turban was in the row in front of me, and as he was getting settled into his seat, I whispered in his ear, "In regards to your inquiry, I'm a hostage. I have no idea why I am here, and I'm from the planet Nebula." Hearing myself say what I said, it had an aura of intrigue and mystery. Diplomatic espionage. Vague yet politically absurd. This *Bush-shit* rubs off.

My turbaned friend immediately began to stroke his beard—again! It's the international code of intellectuals and decision maker and half-baked dysfunctional terrorist. Half glancing over his right shoulder, he coyly smiled, asking, "What planet?" There was an impish gleam in his eye. Sort of like Santa Claus. I thought to myself, *This is deep, surreal, a historical moment.* **In the Moment.** Sublime and surreal. Extreme reality. Just the norm . . . being dysfunctional.

In regards to the question, I replied, "Hopefully this planet!" This seemed to delight him. Laughing, he turned completely around in his chair and quipped, "Brilliant!"

The room went dark, and the screen lit up with the movie, entitled, *The Mid-East: The World in Crisis.*

I'll admit it was an interesting documentary. The presentation on a world in crisis was then, as it is today, overwhelming. I was snoring . . . louder than the movie. Good champagne has that effect on me. *Cheers!*

The documentary ended, and people began mixing and mingling again. It strengthened the international feel of an Un-united Nations. Only in America—water and oil on the canvas of a democracy in lockdown. *Cry, freedom!*

I was just about to take another item on a stick when Mr. Turban approached me. He had a stately, elegant, elderly woman draped over one arm while he chomped aggressively on the tidbit hanging on the end of the stick with the other. She was English. She reminded me of the Queen. She was rigid and starchlike. She was smoking indoors. This was the seventies, and secondhand smoke was socially acceptable. Cancer was in . . .

The Queen, with a haughty air, commenced with a litany of international chitchat and diplomacy laced in medieval grandeur. Somewhere over the rainbow, her eyes narrowed, and she looked at me with a piercing look. Then blowing smoke in my face, she commanded me to reflect on the documentary *The Mid-East: The World in Crisis.* This was spoken with the tone of someone of great importance, status, and clout! As she spoke those who were in earshot stopped. They paid attention, and they listened. It was like an old E. F. Hutton commercial. I'm looking around, amazed and astounded! I'm impressed by

Elizabeth's command of the moment. People were hanging on her every word. Breathless, they waited.

Just as I was about to articulate, she spoke again, "I understand your brother was the producer, director, and one of the writers of this extraordinary historical expedition. What's your assessment of his final presentation?" Now all eyes seem to be focused on me. Suddenly, I was E. F. Hutton. Dare I say, "Donald Trump, you're fired!" This was empowering. As I power-gazed the Queen, she dropped her gaze. I could see my brother, Gene, on the fringe of the group gathering around us. He was shaking his head, and his eyes glared. He slid his index finger across his throat. Things seemed to have gotten tense and urgent. I licked my lips, weighing my thoughts carefully.

I spoke frankly and sincerely—from the heart. Clearing my throat and with hushed anticipation, I said, "I felt it was well orchestrated." I saw my brother exhale a sigh of relief, bobbing his head—*Yes!* He gave me the OK signal—thumbs up! Then, continuing, I said, "The cinematography was brilliant." I could feel the enthusiasm of the international gathering rise. They were beaming. You could feel the swelling undercurrent of applause beginning to build. Then I let the air out of their sails with this next commentary. "If this were a presentation for a travelogue, it was exquisite. Par excellence! However, if memory serves me correctly, I was under the delusion this was intended to give insight and a clearer perspective on the Middle East crisis. If that is the case, it has no social relevance."

There was instant silence. E. F. had struck again. I was immediately pulled to the side by my brother, and in no uncertain terms, he told me, "Go! Now! Go downstairs to the Steak and Brew."

He gave me a hundred dollars, then the *Bum's Rush*. the ol' heave ho and away we go! I was shoved out the door, literally, by the security! I heard the door slam and lock behind me! I was ousted! A coup! The *coup dis-grace*. I mean, "Go to the Steak and Brew!"

I took the elevator down and walked out straight into the Steak and Brew. It's me and you. Well, me for sure. You, not yet. The restaurant had a rustic cute, little New York flavor to it. Regular folks with a tourist heart for Manhattan's atmosphere. Business as usual. I saw you—*the apple of my eye*—whizzing about. Very official in your managerial manner. You appeared happy and contented. In the *zone* interacting with the team, your staff, the workers . . . as if in an ensemble of good actors. On the stage of life.

It was exhilarating. It uplifted me and gave me a sense of confidence after my most recent fall from grace. I'm feeling a sense of inclusion as one of the ensemble was attempting to seat me. I told her you were my brother (I love the *brotherhood*—it's in my spiritual DNA). Rather gushing, the young lady gasped, "Come on, really? That's great!" Laughing, she turned and ran toward you, leaving me hanging on the rails.

I could see her excitement as she spoke with you, then you looked up and toward me. It was a quizzical expression like, "My brother?" Then you realized it was me. You smiled and waved, then continued on with your duties. At last, the young lady must have had a revelation as she unhinged me from the railing and seated me. Remarkable!

Finally, you came over. You beamed, appearing genuinely glad to see me. Then again, it could've been shock. You know, *Casablanca*-ed. Of all the gin joints to come to "la vie en rose, c'est la vie" . . . you and me! Steak and Brew on the House! Gotta be a double entendre in there somewhere? We were on—or off . . . Broadway? Who cares? I know it happened.

Do you remember any of this? Or, am I a forgone conclusion? A delirious delusion of self-indulgence, a narcissistic fetish. A Lance Armstrong. A Psychic Clone. You know what I mean? Of course you don't. **U-Never Really Know What . . . *I Mean?*** Do you? Hey! You're still discovering *you!* Self-mastery. A mystery to self. Why? Very few people want to be themselves. That is, their authentic self. Let me rephrase that—very few people *get* to be themselves. Another way of saying that most want to be that which they are not nor can they be, authentically speaking.

I'd be privileged to this insight on another adventuresome trip to New York City. This time travel period was right after Watergate. An unraveling time for America's revelation. The prophesy hasn't stopped yet. The fulfillment . . . it's back! Yakety-yak! In numerological terms, 911: emergency, 411: the sign or the times, 666: you've been warned, 187: DOA! The wages of sin! A dead issue. The fall from grace.

I was in New York's Times Square. I was out canvassing for a theatrical and/or commercial agent. Mostly, I was trying to find work as an actor; and by the grace and hospitable charity of you and Fran, I was given housing with *the Houses*. A place to stay. *Su casa, mi casa.* Got a green card? The family ass-sociation has benefits. Legal aliens *Welcome.* earthling.com!

This was an authentic revelation time as Sly Stone said, "Thank you fo' let'n me be myself again." And I'll be darned if I didn't get the dual agent I needed. I signed with Black and Beautiful. A **2'fer** all wrapped up as one. Self-realization. Quite empowering. God's will being done! Goodwill.

Settled and signed, I was sitting in your living room meditating and conversing with my higher consciousness. Inspired, I began to write and listen to some tunes on the radio. The music was a funk-fusion groove with a silver throated smooth-talkin' deejay who never failed to let you know "You're listening to the Voice of Darkness coming yo' way with the grooves to move ya! And make you sway. I hope yo' night was as good as yo' day. If not, get on your knees and pray. This is the Voice of Darkness." Then, the groove would go to a funkier level and the Voice would yell, **"Funk it up!"**

As I sat in your living room by myself, groovin' to the Voice of Funk and reason, I could hear your key unlock the front door. As you made your entrance into the living room, your mood was a study in *serious funk*. More *moody blues*. A cloud of funk hung over you like a veil of gloom.

Your voice had the tone of spiritual doom. I stake my case on your behavior with Sarah. Exhibit A, B, C, know what I mean, counselor?

Sarah, your dog. A mixed German shepherd mongrel. An astonishingly beautiful dog. Truly, a lady. So sensitive and extremely intelligent and gentle. Very responsive with her love. You could see it in her eyes. She was family. In fact, she was another minority *Clumpster* to really express true love for me . . . freely. No strings attached. Love is like that. *Wuff . . . wuff . . .*

Sarah had been with me the whole time I was grooving with the Voice. She seemed to enjoy and respect where my spirit was going. It's like she not only knew but understood I was in *my zone.* So she left me alone. She made me feel at home.

It was through Sarah I would get a peep into your frustration of not being your authentic self. I actually saw into your private space where there is no race in your closet. Where you had withdrawn and shrunk and tightly closed the door. Never to be seen. The public would meet a representative of your self. Not your authentic self—the real you. No! Never! Correction . . . *almost* never.

However, by a quirk of fate *and who knows predestination,* somehow the closet door was opened. Keyed by Sarah's joy. The joy of trying to cheer you up. You know, animals sense human hurt—physically, psychologically, and always spiritually. Sarah sensed your gloom and doom in full bloom. A combustible, compressed human meltdown by the light of the silvery moon! When one can't be their authentic self, kick the dog!

That's what I felt as I saw you enter the living room. Although you didn't kick Sarah, you displayed a nasty anger! When Sarah bounded joyously, jumping up and down on you ecstatically because she was really excited to see you, you responded by grabbing the side of her neck or dog collar. I'm a little foggy there, but I remember the tone of harshness in your voice. The sound of frustration. The suppressed irritation being released. Life's stored baggage packed and formulated in childhood, now an emotional regurgitation.

Sarah wasn't the issue nor the topic. She was the object of the negative energy you projected when you yelled, "Get down, Sarah!" It penetrated to the bone, your tone. Sarah dropped down like she was shot! She looked at you like "What dah . . . ?" My head popped up with the same look as Sarah—the "what dah . . . ?" look.

I sat there with my mouth hanging open. Because you always came off sort of milk toast, Deputy Dawg, Huckleberry Hound, Dudley Do-Right, but now, Pandora's Box had opened and revealed *the Enforcer*, snidely whiplashing. Which validates the saying "Looks are deceiving."

That's how Sarah looked. Deceived. No, she looked more like a hurt child—that hurt look children get when they've been waiting all day to play with a parent. When they impulsively run and jump up on you (the parent), the parent with, an edge of rejection in their voice, yells, "Get down."

The child is crushed. That's how Sarah looked. She showed it to me as she walked over and started licking my hand. I looked her right in the eyes. I saw nothing but forgiveness in their loving reflection. It was very humane. This was a celestial moment. Beautiful lady, *Ms. Sarah House!*

Just for a moment, time not only came to a tranquil halt but had become a serene stillness. Silence drowned out sound. I could hear nothing, but the deafening sound of silence crying out. When you sit still and be quiet and let God, it's rather hypnotic Most disarming. Peace. God's will being done through love. Quite a pleasant comfort. To one's spirit. Serenity.

Somewhere during my silent, celestial communion with God, Sarah stood up on my knees, kissed me, then licked my face. She got down and laid on the floor, her eyes beckoning me. They revealed the same look as Daisy. Love. Universal. The law.

I joined Sarah on the floor. She lay on her back and revealed her underside. She wanted me to touch her. I rubbed her gently with a firm hand, sincere and respectful. She opened her heart and became desirous of my petting. Her openness and love humbled me. We tossed, turned, and frolicked in a loving, wholesome way with the grace of our mutual *life force* bonding us. God's will being done for all that has life.

Suddenly, Sarah sighed. She looked me in the eyes, turned, and looked at you. Then she returned her look back to me. She licked my face. She seemed to smile and wink.

I smiled, and tears came to my eyes. We bonded. We were soul mates. Life really is beautiful. The circle the cycle of life!

Sarah looked relieved. She knew I knew. The frustration in you, the inner conflict, turmoil in the family, the pain, she knew. After all, she'd lived there like a child. Animals pick up the vibes.

Our bonded spiritual display of caring touched you deeply. You saw it. It was a transformational moment. It was when your authentic self started the transition. Like the Beauty and the Beast. The transitional process keyed and stimulated by the aura of love that Sarah and I were sharing. So powerful was the moment it clearly overwhelmed you. So strongly did it entice you that you wanted to be enveloped and submerged in it, to be a part. You wanted to come and share in this love. Love has no defense, race, or sexual agenda. Love is the key. It inspired your authentic self to *open the door,* and you came out. You were out and delightfully on. Smiling your candid camera/Kodak moment smile. It was a special moment.

Smiling and beaming a glow of freedom, you got the celebration started. You got a tray of snacks, beer, and wine. Although it was apparent you didn't need a drink. You just needed to be you. A sobering thought. For you were already "Steak and Brewed."

I can still see us—you, Sarah, and I on the carpet, like the best of friends. Best of men, best of peace—*born again!* To talk in love. Loving ye one another as Our Father does. It's a nurturing concept—God's love. It gives birth to his wisdom. Pure understanding—born again! Alive! Wisdom.

She's a tree of life to those who take hold of her. Those
who retain her.

Proverbs 3:18

Sarah was content as she lay between us. Sarah
reminded me of how much women love to hear men talk
peacefully amongst themselves. It brings inner peace and
a tranquil mind to a woman's soul. It secures her spiritual
being when honor and respect is a man's desire. Sarah loved
us both that night. *Ms. Sarah House.* Rest in peace. Thank
you and good night!

This night which was starting to creep into the wee
hours. Hours evaporated literally unnoticed because you
had my undivided attention. I was listening intently.
Hanging on to every word spoken. You were pouring your
bottled up self out. The more you talked, the more intently
I listened. For this was the first and the last time I would be
privileged to hear or see your authentic self. So open and
honest. So free. Truth is like that.

I was taken aback—amazed really—when I learned
you wanted to be a musician, a singer. A band man. You
were an *in-the-closet, rock-'n'-roll dreamer.* You lamented as
I watched you anguish. Anguish about not giving yourself
that option—of making the effort and attempting the
impossible! You'd let the flower fall and blow away and
the *what-if* cloud of doom darken your dream. Your eyes
are your windows to the soul, and I saw vividly that you'd
folded your hopes up and stowed them in the closet, deep
in the closet, forevermore. I rest my case.

Time had really tweaked, and it was taking its toll. You were very fatigued and blurry eyed. Quite woozy from drink and lack of sleep. You thanked me for listening. You hugged me affectionately and kissed me—on the forehead! Do you remember any of this? I sure do. Authentic self is like that . . . divine purpose. **It is written . . .**

Weddings seem to be our thing—our place. The full circle of life—the beginning—**us** in the same place. This time it was Kenny Biter's wedding. This is where I met the new addition to the Houses—Walter. In fact, he and I danced. I believe he was nine. He was a sweet spirit . . . vulnerable and so precious. He reminded me of you. I could hear the creaking door of his *authentic self* starting to close. Abandonment, then adoption can have an unsettling effect, especially on a child.

And finally, the true full circle . . . the defining moment, Nate da' Great's wedding to Mary. Nate and Mary. It was a lovely and beautifully performed ceremony—a yuppie, yippy, hippie flavor. Yet there was a hint of *The Waltons* ala *Little House on the Prairie.* Add to that, some fun-kay *Brady Bunch,* and then of course, I was the *House Spice,* a little *Shaft,* a touch of Black Moses, smoothed over with *Martin, Malcolm* and *Super Fly*—**Da' Man!** Your humble servant!

Still, it was all good seeing so many of *the Clumpsters* cluster in the celebration of a new edition to *the family ass-sociation* in the law of *love.*

The reception was great. With the wonderful array of food and drinks, and the music was slamming. I believe Rick James and James Brown set the pace. And

Lady Isabella Berkeley, all of five or so, picked me as her dancing partner. I remember cameras clicking. The chief photographer, Clare Sullivan, was kept busy clicking away. I recall looking down at Lady Isabella Duncan cutting steps with me, making me feel, for a moment, like Bill Bojangles Robinson dancing with Shirley Temple. All we needed at that point was Michael Jackson singing "On the Good Ship Lollipop."

Finally, the reception shifted to the Houses' Ponderosa out on South Chester Road in Swarthmore. It was here *the Clumpsters* were clustering. This was my third time at the Swarthmore homestead where I initially met *Nate the Sheriff* and was placed under *house arrest!* This time it was informal. Social rather than official sheriff business.

At last, I was free to move about without being dogged by the local constabulary. Although Nate is no longer sheriff. He still has *da' gun!* Hmm.

The House Ponderosa festival was warm, glowing with love. You were running back and forth from cellar to yard and up the back steps through the screened porch into the house. Serving, replacing, and replenishing whatever was needed. You were all over the place. It was the Steak and Brew you. This time, however, you were managing the home front, keeping the par-tay goin'.

Besides celebrating and toasting Nate da' Great becoming one with ol' Mary don'cha weep, we were collectively mourning the passing and the loss of a very wonderful young soul. A soul who had touched many in a short span of life. Shawn Biter. Our darling nephew. Rube and Carol Biter's precious child. **May He Rest in Peace.**

We said approximately ten words through this whole family historical event. Really . . . the full circle, for you always were the silent, strong type. Know what I mean? Naw . . .

U-Never Really Know What . . . *I Mean!*

The Mind Is a Trick-e Place 2 Live

We, as a world, a society, and an individual, live in our mind. It's where we house our thoughts. It's where we do our thinking. It's the place where we store memories, hopes, dreams, and ambitions. Even hate and terrorism, but mostly love.

The mind is a place of refuge. A shelter. A place where we conceive and create our goals, our desires, or fears and where we place our faith. The mind is a retreat, a place of privacy. It's where one's self is maintained, sustained, or destroyed. Living in the mind can be a very *trick-e* proposition for the human spirit. Especially if you get lost in the space of the mind. It can have great psychological ramifications. And the outcome can be devastating. Then again, the mind also has the ability to preserve our state of mind through mental or telepathic perseverance. A positive state of mind. A mental steadfastness. The reassurance that life is good. This is a mind-set.

A mind-set, or a set mind, are terms to confirm the minds capability to transmit these complex elements to the human head or brain. The brain, an organism where the mind is thought to live or die. This mind thing is about life and death. And there are a lot of *"deadheads"* set in their mind's way. A terrorist holds a fanatical self-righteous mind-set or viewpoint. A dead issue to a dead head.

Dead heads are ruining the world. Dead heads who hold high rank and powerful positions in religion and politics. They are easy to detect. They resemble TALKING HEADS. Blah, blah, blah.

After giving much thought to all of this, it prompted me to pose to myself this question: Is our mind really ours? As Arsenio Hall might say, "Hmm!"

Let's be real. All my life, well, nearly all of it, I recall hearing people say unequivocally that their mind told them what to do. What ever it said, they did. Attack! Retaliate! Their mind told them! Attack! Retaliate!

Now this is just me, but it sounds like they are implying "the mind" is a director, a coworker, a joint production. A Spike Lee-type mentality. Dig?

This is mind-blowing! I mean, it boggles the mind! This definitely calls for considerable in-depth attention. There is an aura of great significance, of spiritual importance about all of this. I feel the sense or need to rebut or at least a need to examine more closely the institutionally taught concept of how the world has educated us to view and use our minds. Or, is it perhaps brainwashing? ***In the Moment!*** Terrorism—a Manchurian candidate.

The terror of terrorism is **In the Moment** in that it spews out, unpredictably, violently and maliciously by taking life by the balls and twisting until dead. I have decided that **In the Moment**, I'm going to, in greater depth, listen to people when I hear them say, "My mind said it. I heard some'm in my mind say, 'Kill 'em.'"

A mind so directed can justifiably say, "Kill!" Or, rape, molest, hate, destroy, reject, love, care, join, follow or console, etc. Who knows? Attack? Retaliate? Hmm.

Seriously! Who really knows? Positively? And regardless, we still have to be responsible. We're held accountable, and the mind doesn't mind who knows! Or, who doesn't. It makes for a very *if-e* resolution. The result is like a magicians act. Losing one's mind through illusion or through trick-E deception. Abracadabra. Peekaboo! Is it real, or is it Memorex? My mind or your mind? Do you mind?

It goes without saying. Who knows how vast the vacuum of the mind is? Avoiding trash is man-D-tory; otherwise, the void becomes the mind. Void of matter, except electrical energy triggering spontaneous and explosive thoughts. Thoughts that ignite the night sky—in yo' head. It happens to me, even while asleep in my bed.

One time while asleep, one of those serene, peaceful sleeps, I found that I was not asleep! I was in my mind, *wide-awake!* I could see the nature of *understanding*. Because I could hear it, and what I heard made perfect sense. I could see it unfold . . . the truth of the mind. The revealing of creativity. It was like walking in space. I'm walking in darkness yet, there is light. Light reflecting in the dark. Or within the dark of the mind, there is light!

I heard a voice coming from out of the dark light within the mind, saying, "Look-EE dare! That li'l boy is a man! But you still dat li'l boy. Mickey, you was a bright child. Knew all kinds of stuff beyond your years. Just born smart and gifted."

The more I listened, the more recognizable was the voice. I began laughing, and I said, "Aunt Elsie . . . Aunt Elsie!" The light suddenly diminished, down to almost what appeared to be a lightening bug or firefly. It began to flutter, then took off! It looked like a miniaturized comet. It's little tail streaked through the darkness. Then bursting into a huge bright light. It was like watching a fireworks display. Then like zillions of microscopic light particles, the light dispersed into air.

I watched the light particles slowly and majestically descend like falling snow flakes and form into a shape of a person. And there she was *AUNT ELSIE!* She had a big smile on her face, her eyes were bright like the light she came out of. The last time I saw her she was old, tired, broken down, and probably legally blind. Her teeth were in bad shape. She was frail.

I was in Boston when she passed. I wasn't at her funeral. As a kid, I used to leave church early. Sometimes, I didn't even go but just go over to see Aunt Elsie and Uncle Bubbles, Aunt Elsie's husband. They were, for me, a real-life vaudeville comedy act. A routine. They were a blend of George Burns and Gracie Allen. The *Honeymooners*. Add the spice and color of George "Kingfish" Stevens and his wife, Sapphire, of Amos 'n' Andy, mix it up, and you'd have Aunt Elsie and Uncle Bubbles! They were the greatest gift a child could have.

"Mickey . . ." It was the sound of Aunt Elsie's voice that snapped me back into the present—or the presence of the mind. It started to sink in. It's Aunt Elsie, and she's looking wonderful! In fact, she looked a lot like Ethel Waters did in *Cabin in the Sky*. You know, that Southern flavored, fresh off the plantation *Gone with the Wind* Aunt Jamima look. ***In the Moment!*** *Classics!* The mind . . . when it's beautiful! When it's godsend . . . is ***In the Moment!***

Aunt Elsie's skin looked youthful and clear. Not a blemish or wrinkle on her face. Her eyes sparkled. She smiled, and her teeth were immaculate—flawless. Her teeth, like the light of her eyes, gleamed. Everything about her seemed bright and full of light. She was literally glowing. Then angelically, she stepped out of the light and lit up the darkness of my mind.

In a blink of an eye, we are standing in Lincoln Courts, a housing project for moderate to low income tenants. It looked the way it did before white people came back to reclaim the urban city. The same city they had run from years ago in *white flight*. It's sort of a social irony, the return of the white people. Regentrification. It's a "here today and gone tomorrow" principle—a return to capture the inner city. *The Mas-tah returns.* Still the benevolent despot—masters of the universe, white supremacy, *the lords of London,* the Princeton skull and crossbone of Wall Street. *Eh, Bernie Madoff!*

And Lord have mercy, here I am, standing in Lincoln Courts with Aunt Elsi—live and in *living colors!* A light reflects in my mind, amidst everything else, leaving me razzled and dazzled! Aunt Elsie is alive! That was the one thought I couldn't shake, and is this real? or is this a dream? It sure feels real to me. I feel wide-awake and ***In the Moment!***

I scratch my head and begin to rub my eyes. I can see a beautiful blue sky, the cyclone fenced-in grassy area. The deep cranberry, four-story building of Lincoln Courts where Aunt Elsie and Uncle Bubbles lived on the fourth floor. Their living room window and bathroom window faced out onto the courtyard. They had a modest one bedroom. It was in this cozy haven of love I was thoroughly amused and entertained by Elsie and Bubbles. What an act. What a blessing. *Thank You, God!*

It was Uncle Bubbles who orchestrated the mood and tempo of *The Show.* Showtime always started as soon as I walked into the apartment—Uncle Bubbles would say, "My man!" and Aunt Elsie would immediately come over from the stove.

The stove was a family tradition. She was always putting a pot on the stove. "Got to have a pot ready at all times. You never know who's gonna show up . . . unexpectedly! And you'se got 2 B Rea-Dee!" Aunt Elsie always said. "Ain't nobody jus' gonna pop in! And can't get som' em. I always got som'em to give. Look at my cute li'l baby!"

A statement like that would bring Uncle Bubbles right out of his racing forum. Uncle Bubbles was very exacting when it came to thoroughbreds. He said I was one. He was an expert. He was an *exercise boy* who wanted to be a jockey. But sadly, he grew a little too big and too heavy! So he got to exercise the horses—not race! He had great insight on *The Race.*

Ironically, I believe deep down, that's why Aunt Elsie married him. He was the closest thing to a jockey she could get . . . *on the rebound!* 'Cause Uncle Bubbles was Aunt Elsie's *second* husband. Her first husband, Charles Winkfield, a late nineteenth-century jockey. His last race in America was between 1908 and 1912. Then he moved to France because of *The Race Card,* and he was off!

In the beginning of thoroughbred racing, the majority, if not all, the major jockeys were black. In fact, at the first Kentucky Derby, twelve out of fifteen jockeys were black. That's why there are **black jockeys** on people's front lawns. They were hitching posts in the days when horses provided public transportation. And, at first, this was an honor.

With Uncle Bubbles, race or black jockeys weren't the issue. It was Aunt Elsie and her concept of me. *Elsie! Now* . . . wait a minute. As Uncle Bubbles spoke, I could hear in the tone of his voice, he was no *exercise boy.* Uncle Bubbles was a lot like Uncle Remus. He had a way with children. Especially me! I vividly recall Uncle Bubbles reaching down and lifting me up onto his knees—that is, before I got to big and heavy. He'd then begin telling me about Hollywood and about the things, which constituted the rites of passage. Things that sanctioned your rights to be a part of Hollywood. He would say, "You got all the attributes for Hollywood. Smart and entertaining. You're debonair, suave, and smooth. You're like Fred Astaire. You're dressed to a T. suit, shirt, and tie. Cuff links too. Shoes so shiny they look like patent leather. I can almost see my face in 'em."

Uncle Bubbles would then pick my hat up and place it gently on my head, careful to adjust it by bending the brim over my right eye. Then squinting his eyes, much like a jeweler looking at a rare and precious jewel. Tugging at his bottom lip with his index finger and thumb, furrowing his brow, tilting his head to the right, and presto! The light of genuine creative genius would *flash!*

Uncle Bubbles would get up, slide me off his knee, and go over to the break front cabinet. He'd reach into a drawer and pull out two sets of black sunglasses. Put a set on me, and the other he'd wear. Then he would give the *official declaration* of my destiny: "You are going to Hollywood! You're a star! Smile, you're on *candid* camera!"

We'd both bust out in uncontrollable laughter. Uncle Bubbles got such a kick out of watching me having a *laughing orgasm.* I was truly in my natural environment. Pure joy in being appreciated and respected. Uncle Bubbles, like many of the adults in my early childhood experiences, gave me my props. They recognized me as a *person.* A gift to them, and as far as I could see, they were a gift to me! I always understood my blessings in people **In the Moment** as Love and God's will being done. Blessed are the *doers!*

Right about this moment, Aunt Elsie would come in with her *Elsie shit!* It was the pivotal point of the juxtaposition to the routine. This is what made the act work. So sweet . . . *Aunt Elsie's shit.* Aunt Elsie would always come in with a high-pitched voice and take the groove to another level. Her timing was impeccable.

She'd start in right at the height of our joyous, natural high—*me* falling down with laughter, and Uncle Bubbles doubled over coughing and laughing! His mouth open, *coughing!* His tongue folded over—going in and out of his mouth—as he coughed. Like one of those Happy New Year curled paper horns you blow at midnight. Except it was more like *LAST CALL*, party's over!

To me, *Aunt Elsie's shit* came off like a bust. Her voice was like a shrill siren! Warning us she was about to change the groove. It was now **her show!** She knew how to upstage, taking the SPOTLIGHT off of me and Uncle Bubbles. She was *da' ruler* **and** *da' diva*. Her words hit our joy like Ali's phantom punch hit Sonny Listen. Hitting us as I fall on the floor, and Uncle Bubbles coughs, gags with his veins a-pop'n out of his head, and his tongue rolling in and out of his mouth, while *Aunt Elsie's shit* continued to pile it on.

As she began to dictate the facts of reality, she holds up the Bible, making this official! Then she'd begin by saying, "See there, Bubbles, you lying so much! You gagging yourself. The Lord's trying to help you. And . . . save the baby from all yo' BS gagging you, choking off yo' foolishness. You better take heed 'fore the Lord leaves your butt here, all gagged and choked. And stop filling that boy's head with all that Hollywood foolishness! That boy ain't going to no damn Hollywood! And neither are you! And take them damn glasses off. Ain't no damn sun in here. That boy's gonna get a good job, like his daddy. Get an education. Make some' em' out of his self. So! Stop filling his head with all that Hollywood nonsense. Besides, Hollywood is a dream for white people." This was, the early fifties.

That statement hit a nerve! Psychologically, it almost rocked my belief system. Because even though I was blessed with a great deal of joy and spontaneous fun, Uncle Bubbles had implanted a serious thought in me, and Aunt Elsie just threw a curve ball right into the middle of my *dream.*

Uncle Bubbles was more serious than Aunt Elsie could have ever imagined. For she'd long since stopped believing in that type of **dreaming.** The vision placed in the mind, and if truly believed, diligently pursued by faith and trust in God, it **can** become a reality. For where, there is, no vision. People perish!

Uncle Bubbles was a very intuitive person, and he had a keen and perceptive spirit. A *sixth sense*, you might say. Before Aunt Elsie's cloud of gloom could settle in, Uncle Bubbles, like the improv veteran he was, saved the show by throwing some offbeat, abstract humor into the mix. With a straight face, he would simply state, "Elsie! It ain't about being white. White ain't really no—big-El" Then turning to me with that mystical gleam in his eye, smiling and with a nod of his head and wink of his eye, he would drop the **bomb!**

"Elsie! For your information, I was originally white. At birth. But! My mama dipped me in a barrel of water, with a bunch of rusty ole nails. So we still goin' to Hollywood. What da' hell!"

I remember one time, Uncle Bubbles *played the broom*, which was really a unique virtuoso performance. Actually, all of Uncle Bubbles's talents were executed with great efficiency 'cause I never could figure out how he got that broom to make a musical sound. Someway he'd rub that broom over the edge of the kitchen table and with the broom held between his fingers, like a pool player, he'd somehow slide the broom back and forth. Sliding through his fingers and over the table, he'd apply a little pressure, like an upright base player slides his bow. And the sound of a base fiddle hum would blend into Uncle Bubble's melodic humming.

Then Uncle Bubbles would show his versatility and artistic dexterity by getting his spoons and his bones and play them off himself. He'd hold them like a drummer holds his drumsticks, and then he'd manipulate them with his fingers, getting them to *click, clack, cling*. He really got all worked up, sweating. He'd make vocal sounds that provided a sort of harmonic accompaniment. It was truly a sight.

For his finale, it was the playing of a steel washboard while singing "Yankee Doodle Came to Town." By this time, Uncle Bubbles was trip'n on his natural high, and I was high right along with him! I'd be dancing, singing, and waddling in all this love and joy. I knew it was love. I was **In the Moment!**

It had to be love because it got to Aunt Elsie. She was dancing, wiggling, and then started doing the Black Bottom, a dance of her generation and time. She looked so happy and so contented.

Once, me and Uncle Bubbles were really trip'n when he got so excited, he yelled, "**Holly-wood! Woo-woo! WOOD! Hol-ly . . . wood!**" He then looked at me, stuck his hands out, palms up for me to slide some skin. As my hands slid over his, he smiled affectionately with glee in his eyes. Then he'd say, "Man! 'Cause you'ses a li'l man . . . CAT DADDY, you're perfect for Hollywood. You're a player. Put yo' sunglasses on!"

No matter how blissed and blessed his revelation, Aunt Elsie would still do her *Elsie shit!* I truly believe it was the straightforward and honest character of Aunt Elsie that gave our act its authenticity. The yin in the yang!

Aunt Elsie was always on cue with her *Elsie shit*, hitting us at the top of our game. Banging the kitchen table, she would yell, "Bubbles! Stop it with this Holly-Wood! WOOD-Woo! Hollywood. I told you that boy ain't going to no damn Holly-WOOOOd. He keep learning all this foolishness from you! And he won't even go across the street. Let alone, Hollywood. Next, you'll be tell 'em to go to Hollywood and pick som' cotton."

Then she turned and walked back to the stove to stir, or flip, or do whatever she would do to whatever it was she was cooking. Usually, it was some kind of fish, cabbage greens, or some'm good. By this time, instead of upstaging and taking the spotlight from Aunt Elsie, Uncle Bubbles would have thought up a clever comeback. "Elsie! You can scoff and mock me, but who knows? He might be able to pick cotton in Hollywood. After all, Hollywood did make *Cotton Comes to Harlem*."

That was the show! That is to say, to the best of my memory, it was ***In the Moment!*** I realized then that I'd traveled into the past, to Lincoln Courts, to Uncle Bubbles, me and Aunt Elsie, standing ***In the Moment!*** where darkness meets the light. She stood there smiling and gently clapping like an audience who had just seen a fabulous performance, "Bravo! Fantastico!"

As I stood ***In the Moment!*** I felt it pass and about to run out! Evaporate! Puff! Poof! I recall looking to the sky, and yes, there was a sky in the darkness of my mind. But the joy of being ***In the Moment!*** lit the skylight, lighting up my mind and enlightening my soul. There ***In the Moment!*** I saw Aunt Elsie looking so elegant and divine.

Without so much as a second thought, I inquired, "Aunt Elsie, how does it feel . . . to be . . . dead? I had no idea what her response would be. Only I knew whatever it would be, it would be impeccable and precise. She was a showstopper! She chuckled and amusingly said, "I don't know. I ain't dead . . ."

That was definitely not the response I had anticipated. I'm standing there shaking my head, like I have Tourette's syndrome. My head nervously ticking. My verbalization somewhat uncontrollable. It's like they're not my words, or the way I would usually word or phrase what I heard myself saying, "Aunt Elsie, if you ain't dead, how come they buried you?" **Oops!**

Aunt Elsie was very amused. She didn't waste any time with a reply. In fact, she was in hysterics. She was laughing so hard, but she got the answer out anyway. "Boy! I mean, Man! Mic-key, you always had a funny way of getting to the truth. Had to tell you the truth. Pure and simple. You love the truth, the whole truth. The truth is that wasn't me they buried! That was the shell of me. The dust, and we all got to go back to where the shell of us came. But the real us, the part that belongs to God, that part we call life and what belongs to God gets to go back. God reaps what God sows. This is the life after death. A reality. Only life is real, and life belongs to God. So! I live with God. This is why you should believe in God. To conquer death."

I had to let this revelation sink in. I felt reduced to a child. It was in an almost childlike manner I posed my next question, "Aunt Elsie, have you seen the Lord?: She smiled a warm, compassionate smile, then in a very matter-of-fact way answered, saying, "All the time!"

Now I am really beside myself. I can hardly contain my enthusiasm. I blurted out, "What does God look like?" She replied, "Indescribable. You'll have to see God for yourself. And you will."

She smiled as I watched her standing there. She was beaming. It was an angelic glow coming out of the joy and understanding of what she was telling me. Then impulsive questions began to explode into my mind. The next thing I knew, I'd blurted out, "Aunt Elsie, who's there in heaven with you? Besides the Lord. Any people I might know?"

She didn't respond right away. She took a moment or two to smooth out her dress. She tugged slightly on her apron and patted the side of her head. I could literally see the words forming on her lips and resounding in my ears. "Yo' mama! Uncle Redd, Mama Lelia. All kinds of yo' people—God's family. Tim, Jim, Hosea, Orlee, Fats, Uncle Johnny, Bones, El, Lucile, Lorain, Jake! Bubbles and Tony too! Truly wonderful and Big Scotty too! You'll see them all again. When it's your time, Mickey."

I cleared my throat, and somewhat hesitantly, I said, "Oh yeah, my name is Mick **E.**, not Mic-**key**!" Aunt Elsie placed her hand on her hips, turned her head to the right, almost appearing to look over her right shoulder as she gradually turned around, and scratching the side of her face, she said, "Why you go and change yo' name?"

I realized that was a straight line, the setup. So I said to myself, "Self, it's showtime," and I quipped, "I changed my name because of people, mostly white people, they kept confusing me with the famous Mickey—THE MOUSE! So I changed my name to Mick **E.**" We laughed and she seemed to be taking *In the Moment!* She broke the moment with a declaration, "I have to admit, Bubbles was right. He said you were going to Hollywood. SHOWTIME . . . *word up!* Let your light shine. The world needs a performance of love. Heaven here on earth, Mick E.!" She beamed a majestic glow. An aura of love!

Then Aunt Elsie embraced me by placing her head on my shoulder, saying, "You're such a joy. And a pleasure to God! God loves you! Now! Sing me a song." I was very flattered and kissed her gently on the forehead. In a hushed voice, I said, "Aunt Elsie, I can't sing! I am not a singer." Her head popped up and off my shoulder. She looked me dead in the eyes. Her forehead furrowed, she squinted her eyes, and with a Delia Reese *Touched by An Angel* look, she said, "I'm tell'n you, this is not a request, Li'l Mickey! Mick E. or whatever! I didn't ask you if you were a singer. I said, sing me a song . . . please!" Aunt Elsie was aglow, and her words had the tone of chastisement. I could hear it in her voice. I shook my head and laughed. She was still a *showstopper.* Tugging at my ear, I said, "What song?"

Aunt Elsie closed her eyes and made her request, which was "Ebb Tide." It was Uncle Bubbles's favorite song. I began to sing the song, and Aunt Elsie cuddled close to me, nestling her head on my shoulder. When I finished singing, she looked at me, her eyes twinkled, and the tears streamed lovingly down her face. There was so much joy behind those precious tears. And as suddenly as in the beginning, Aunt Elsie became a bright light. In the dark. And with a burst and flash, *WHOOSH!* She was gone!

I sat up in my bed wide-awake. I thought, *Was that real? Was this my mind,* or is it **In the Moment!** Hmm. Where's Arsenio Hall now? Perhaps he's ***In the Moment!*** Hmm . . .

At this point, I got out of bed and marched myself straight down to the living room and sat down at the dining room table. I got my yellow legal pad and my friend *da' pen* and wrote this:

THE MIND IS A TRICK-E PLACE 2 LIVE

DEATH: A SUBTLE REMINDER 2 LIVE!

Oh, my Lord, my Lord! My Lord God, the merciful.

—Anonymous

I remember these words over and over, every time I go to a funeral, or hear of a funeral . . . then *snap!* I hear my mother saying, "People always make erroneous living testaments and vows of not letting another day go by without keeping in closer contact and being more conscious of friends, family, and neighbors. Of course, doing the will of God, they say all that. Then go home and go to sleep. The next day, they wake up with convenient amnesia. When will they just wake up and just do it? Before it's their turn to be the dead. Can't they understand it's death trying to tell them about life. So live while you can. And die when you can't help it."

My mother got that final point from Mama Lelia, my father's mother. Mom is the word. Whew! My mother and grandmother were so right on! Now I can really hear what they meant in regards to the message of death. Death is inevitable. *Oh, ev'vabody got to die!* Death's an inheritance that we must live through to die. Die so that we can be reborn in Christ. We are just travelers on the road to heaven. Our passports read Citizen of Heaven, not of earth. So we return, just like we were when we came into the world.

Spiritually dead—this is what we say of the lawless, the materialist, the idolater. It's obvious by these words we don't want to go through life, like driving a car through a red light. We can only go through life in the truth of the way, which is in Christ Jesus. The master and conqueror of life after death—Christ, the Light. The passage from the darkness of death to the light of life. It's very subtle, and it's the purpose behind the resurrection of Christ Jesus. Physical death is not the answer; it is your spiritual rejuvenation—in being born again! Now we can kick death in the butt, rejoicing at the funeral, yelling, "Death! Where is thy sting!"

That's deep! The subtleness of the revelation of God's will, God's love for us revealed in the coffin bed of death. Because death, like the bread of life, must be eaten. People know this in the symbolic, academic, and theological sense. Nevertheless, it's in the spirit realm people lack the understanding of what the allegory of the tree of knowledge really means and why death is the reminder to live.

Death is a subtle and visual effect of this world. The effect of the Tree of Knowledge without the understanding of the Lord's divine will and purpose for our life. A life like this is devoid of spiritual substance. When we accept the Lord's gift of life, it would be wise to live it according to his will, or we'll keep passing on the spore of death, the intruder and interrupter of the flow of life. Everyone has access to the knowledge of God's will—through listening to the spirit within. Yes, we have that knowledge but absolutely not a clue of understanding. Even the mustard-seed-of-faith folk know "knowledge of God's will with no understanding equals death."

God spoke to man, saying, "You shall **not** eat of every tree in the garden. Especially the fruit of the tree of knowledge of good and evil, which is in the midst of the garden." God said, "You shall not eat it, nor shall you touch it lest you die. For God knows that in the day you eat of the fruit, your eyes will be opened, and you will be like God knowing good and evil."

That was paraphrased from Genesis 3:1-3, 6. According to this scriptural allegory, we have inherited the ability to know good. And we also equally know evil. Unfortunately, we have the knowledge and not an ounce of understanding. The knowledge that is of God, with no understanding, will get us killed. Like *dead!* We know good and evil. The catch is we don't spiritually know right from wrong. Now! Will we confess that without God's gift of life in Christ, lived out through us? We dead?

Therefore, I have deduced that I personally feel death is trying to explain our degradation into hell, and Christ is trying to lead us up into our gift from God, *new life in Christ, born-again.*

Death does not discriminate, and it will visit everybody. See, death knows there's always trouble in the flesh. It **is** the wage of sin. The sins of the fathers recycled through the loins of the mother. The next generation of boys and girls of the fallen, and we are that world. Merchants of death. A dead issue for our children. They can come and go so fast, so wake up everybody and live. You don't want **DEATH** *2-B a subtle reminder 2 live!* This is not a wake-up call, you know. Hell-o? *Hell-o, 911? This is the Lord. Can I help you to live?*

TO A VERY SPECIAL HU-MAN

Reflectively rewritten and revised, an acknowledgment of a regretful awareness of a deeper insight. A serious oversight. An overreaction to why hindsight is never *20/20*.

In a message to all mankind, Christ Jesus gave to us an instructive prayer of discipleship directly concerning children. For he knew man's ability to err and man's inclination to misuse God, *Our Father's*, greatest gift to his children—CHILDREN! The embryo of his image. His son made in the image of man, spoke to his children, saying, "Our Father, hallowed be thy name . . ."

Daddy—God, Our Father—thus, you don't disturb Mother Nature, for when disturbed, you get the wrath of God, *Our Father!* When Mother Nature is off, it creates psychological temptations, hellish illusions of the mind in God's children. *Sex in the City* desperate housewives of Suburbia—Shamless. Their "the new normal" praising the Lord. Com'n in, the name and Satan knows this—and more! Satan has woven religion into the principality of his government and created the divisive nature of church and state. He keeps man at war with himself—killing himself, maiming himself, starving himself, and letting His children die for want of food that is abundant, but under the authority of a psychotic conspiracy of world state and religious institutions. Teaching us to self-destruct. Blasphemy! Sins of the fathers. Recycled through, your mamas, drama! It real scary. "Happy Mother's Day!" This is why you don't mess with Mother Nature.

To screw yo'self—damned if you do, damned if you don't! September 11. Hello? Nevertheless, you still got to pay tithes and taxes. Ain't that a bitch. This is the sin-drome, syn-drome, the fall of man that the sins of the father will be made manifest through yo' mama's drama. This is why evil seems to be winning. It's so vividly expressed through the children who are now suicidal, homicidal, sexually twisted, and totally contaminated by the cultivation of misunderstanding of their spiritual identity with God—*Our Father*, the supreme parent, who stands in conflict with the flesh.

I learned this the hard way. I must confess, but confession is good for the soul. The truth shall set you free! And freely I will share some hindsight restoration by the will of a loving Father—God!

This redemption from hindsight was the piece originally written to and for Toren Michael Jones—a gift. God's child left in my pa-rental trust, and I *almost* messed up the trust. Doing my will instead of God's will—to a very special *hu-man.* And the irony of it all would be *busted in the right by the wrong seed sown.* Seeds of wrong that would bloom in the face of good intention, which paves the way to hell!

So let's travel back in time to January 31, 1997, and the original confessed writing of the piece: *To a Very Special Hu-man.*

Dear Son,

I write to you to reaffirm and rescue you from the spirit of alienation. And you being the scholarly person you are, the intelligent analyst you can be, with a deeper perception beyond your fourteen years. I do not desire to see you become an alien.

Especially with me. In turn, leaving our relationship like an X-File, seriously estranged. We have become as incompatible as water and oil. Alienated.

Alienation! Now the characteristics of our relationship formulated and cloaked by withdrawal and separation masked with a smile. The undertones of a shallow and very hollow interrelationship called father and son.

These notations are the alarm signals, the desperate outcry, and the plea from me to you—for you to hang in there.

I write these alarming pleas stimulated by our conversation the other night when I asked you, "Why is my toothbrush on the floor?"

And you knew I wanted a logical, sound, realistic, and practical response. I'm like that. From my point of view, this wasn't an unreasonable request. Naturally, it's my point of view. But as I watched your facial expressions, the glare, the intensity, I felt the air surrounding me—the aura thicken. Not good! I received all this looking into your eyes—your soul.

Looking into you, I saw it so clearly. I saw a person cornered, trapped, and about to panic. A heartbeat away from freaking out! Even now, I can still see you nervously twitching. It was like watching a fugitive being interrogated and persecuted. A very sad picture. A wake-up call to me.

Well! I am awake! Awake and feeling a deep sadness and a deeper regret. Not guilt. No one is guilty. This is strictly about hidden and suppressed feelings. The truth of the revelation is that I'm feeling those feelings of being exposed to my consciousness. Exposed to about how you truly feel about me.

The bottom line or point in case is, I have made some atrociously serious mistakes with you. And because of these serious atrocities upon your consciousness, you are making seemingly the same misconceptions of me. Only, you have come close to a final judgment. And Crucifixion! There is a small chance for a stay of execution—slim to none. The verdict appears to be: *You don't like . . . me!*

This is how I felt, but it was your response, the words and tone and, of course, your face. The picture is worth a thousand words of confirmation. That this dislike was deeper psychologically than I could ever imagine. Yet! It became crystal clear, clarified by the clever denial of that observation, when I asked you a simple question: "Are you afraid of me?"

You replied, "No."

Searching your *soul reflectors*, your eyes, I could see the flicker of the soul's inner light was low. There was an ember but no flame. No spiritual fire nor desire. Your inspiration was more dead than alive. Zombified! The look of the living dead.

Upon observing this, I rephrased my inquiry. Sitting here as I rewrite this piece, I can even use the term "inquest." A quasi trial. But in self-defense, I softened my investigative approach. I side barred with the kid, sort of off the record.

I said to you, "Do you fear me?"

And your response—my son, was a deliberate obstruction of justice—a felony! Obstruction of the truth, the whole truth, so God can help us. Oh no, you didn't go for help. You responded even slower. So slow, pondering over the loopholes or possible entrapments that would be created with reinstatement of Exhibit A. *Afraid*. Or Exhibit B. *Fear!*

You responded as if to avoid any form of perjury. Ironically, you didn't take the fifth. You courageously and cautiously replied, "No, I am not afraid of you. I don't fear you."

As soon as the words left your mouth and registered in my ears, you looked relieved. And satisfied with your response and relieved of a burden of proof with *the whole truth* having been dodged. Avoiding a very well-placed arsenal of my skills to get a true conclusion or conviction.

Somewhat baffled, I was beginning to feel like a hung jury. This called for a second side bar, this time with *Our Father*, God. Turning to the supreme court, I threw myself on the mercy of his court. Because God knows our heart and is the only one capable of a fair and just assessment. For God is the only one capable of understanding righteous judgment.

So after my side bar with *Our Father*, I subpoenaed the truth, THE WHOLE TRUTH. It seemed like an eternity had passed as words had gone unspoken. But thoughts were being heard and truth was being reflected through the pureness I saw in your eyes.

I could see your growth cycle. Your life up until now passing before me, and I wasn't there. I was the alienation—the problem. The cause of the inquisition.

Momentarily, my brain froze. My mind was on hold. This was deeper than I had anticipated because I was looking at this strictly from my viewpoint. But God, the supreme judge, had revealed and uncovered your point of view. Standing on the statutes of classic jurisprudence—*the sins of the father passed down*—is at fault. Yet by his infinite mercy and grace, this was to be the key to my defense.

Regrouped, I threw down my *Father card* like Johnny Cochran, saying emphatically, "Let me try this. Do I intimidate you?"

That hit a vital nerve. Your eyes lit up like a Christmas tree. Like a video game in a penny—let me rephrase—a dollar arcade. *Tilt.* Your response was immediate and without the slightest hesitation, you said, "Yes."

*Boom! Bingo! Bam! **Jackpot!*** Suddenly, I realized I'd built a case I didn't want to win. Why? To win and lose you? What's the point? If I lose you, I lose myself. The father and the son are one. And to achieve this oneness, there must be a code of honor and trust. The whole truth, upheld and understood by the will of *Our Father,* the law creator of good will. This had to be a win-win situation.

So by the law of good will, God's will being done, I broke you down. I tore down the barriers of fear, afraid, and intimidation, and snatched the mask of gloom off. I reviewed the records.

For the readers, let's explore the records of the court:

Exhibit A: **Fear:**   A strong sense of danger. Afraid, dread, panic, terror.

Exhibit B: **Afraid:**   Filled with fear or apprehension, having dislike for something.

Exhibit C: **Intimidate:**   To make timid or fearful, frightened. To make afraid, terrify, bulldoze, bully, brow beat, or a sense of inferiority into submission to break the spirit.

In conclusion, according to this mock trial, you would've incriminated and perjured yourself. And this would've been the moment the prosecuting attorney would have said the following:

Mr. Toren Michael Jones,

You have stated under oath in a court of law, that you were not afraid of your father. You have no fear of your father.

Yet you unequivocally agree your father is an intimidating factor to your sense of self worth. Which by definition is to "make timid, fearful, frightened or afraid." Therefore, Mr. Jones, it is by your own statement and correct definition that shows you have suppressed your true feelings of borderline hate! Which is derived from fear, anger, dislike, and loathing. Masked by denial.

Which puts your relationship with your father on a fragile basis. And on the endangered species list for the kingdom of God. **Oops, dere it iz!**

I rest my case.

But thank God, *Our Father*, for this is not a mock trial. This is about love, the understanding of the whole truth, be it God's will. His good will in **forgiveness.**

Therefore, I ask of you, if I have made you feel all that has been previously stated, tried, and proved to be the problem—then the PROBLEM is ME! At least it is at the root of why you feel as you do. I am truly and sadly sorry. And I humbly ask your forgiveness. Because if these feelings are not truly dealt with, it can be a very unhealthy psychological and spiritually traumatic living experience. Our life.

For one who has fear, has torment, Scripture states God did not give us fear. God gave us a sound mind and power in his spirit. Love! God's love! And God's love casts fear out. He or she who has fear is not made perfect in love.

And one who is intimidated can't love or embrace the *intimidator.* It's like the pusher and the addict. The pimp and the prostitute. These types of relationships are based on a love-hate relationship. The dark side.

Your eyes are the mirrors to your soul and can't hide or mask the whole truth. The truth is, you have a very difficult time with me! And it is very understandable. But give it time and don't judge and have no fear. Be not afraid. God's love is always near. And let God's love be the light of you in your eyes guiding you through the darkness of your misunderstanding of me. Remember, I have a great deal of respect for your growth and development—spiritually and psychologically.

Peace, my son,

Love, Dad

STUMBLING BLOCKS TO: CHRIST AND HIS PURPOSE

What are the stumbling blocks to Christ, and what are the things that divide believers or those who profess to be believers? Misinterpretation and taking Scripture out of context. These will cause believers to stumble and sometimes fall because of their failure to remember **God is a living God.** They become disillusioned and turn away from their walk with the Lord. We know Satan can't *steal* salvation, but he *can steal* a man's testimony—making him weak and useless as a witness for the Kingdom of God. *Stumbling blocks* are cool tools Satan uses to fool the believer into giving up and turning to false teachers and liars who deceive and confuse.

Misunderstanding opens the way for manipulation of God's word. God's will takes a backseat to the ego's own purpose. Pettiness and pride will surely precede a fall as Satan tells the fallen believer that his agenda is the will of

God. Strife and division leads to chaos and confusion. Mo'
stumbling! Here we go—*loop d' loop.*

Here is what the Scripture says in regards to those
stumbling blocks to the purpose of Christ—the eternal
friend we have in Jesus.

> *For my thoughts are not your thoughts, nor are your*
> *ways my ways, says the Lord. For as the heavens are*
> *higher than the earth, so are my ways, higher than*
> *your ways, and my thoughts than your thoughts.*
>
> Isaiah 55:8-9

The greatest stumbling block that divides God's word
is when the believer claims to know the *Word* and is
supposedly being guided by the *Word,* leading the simple
and ignorant straight to Satan.

> *Now, I urge you brethren, note those who cause*
> *divisions and offenses, contrary to the doctrine which*
> *you learned and avoid them. For those who are such*
> *do not serve our Lord Christ Jesus, but their own*
> *belly, and by smooth words, and flattering speech*
> *deceive the hearts of the simple.*
>
> Romans 16:17-18

> *Now, I plead with your brethren, by the name of our*
> *Lord Christ Jesus, that you all speak the same thing,*
> *and that there be no divisions among you, but be*

perfectly joined together in the same mind and in the
same judgment. Is Christ divided?

1 Corinthians 1:10,13

These are grumblers, complainers, walking according
to their own lusts; and they mouth great swelling
words, flattering people to gain advantage. But you,
beloved, remember the words which were spoken
before by the apostles of our Lord Jesus Christ: how
they told you that there would be mockers in the last
time who would walk according to their own ungodly
lusts. These are sensual persons, who cause divisions,
not having the Spirit. Glory to God, to Christ. Now
to Him who is able to keep you from stumbling, and
to present you faultless before the presence of His glory
with exceeding joy.

Jude 1:16-19,24

All the previously mentioned is a part of the many variations to deceive, misguide, and create pitfalls to our faith in the purpose of Christ Jesus, who died for our sake and was resurrected for our freedom to overcome the world by the empowerment by faith, through our works in Christ, Christ in US, the faithful. The just of sound mind, who live by faith, seen in our daily works. A living example. However, all fall, even the Elect. *Flip-flop!*

Just as a coin has two sides, Jesus, the resurrected Christ Jesus, has two natures. One as Jesus, the son of man. Born into flesh by the immaculate conception yet was not of the flesh. His other nature, his divinity, as the son of God, from whom he descended and came into the flesh to take away man's sin.

It was done miraculously through his sacrificial death, the shedding of his anointed blood and resurrection to life eternal by the conquering of death—the wages of sin—and we all fall short of his glory.

He did this as the closing act of his earthly life for our salvation, redemption, and the abundance of life, then life eternal. And it was finished, completed the fulfillment of prophecy. The word "born-again" as in the beginning. This is why we must be born again in Christ. If we are believers and followers of Jesus, the resurrected Christ. The just, the seeds of Abraham. *The faithful* born again to our original selves.

> *So all this was done that it might be fulfilled, which was spoken by the Lord through the prophet, saying: "Behold the virgin shall be with child, and bear a Son, and they shall call His name Immanuel," which is translated, "God with us."*
>
> Matthew 1:22-23

> *. . . for that which is conceived in her is of the Holy Spirit. And she will bring forth a Son, and, you shall call his name Jesus, for He will save His people from their sins.*
>
> Matthew 1:20-21

In the beginning was the Word, and the Word was with God, and the Word was God. He was in the beginning with God. All things were made through Him, and without Him nothing was made that was made.

John 1:1-3

But as many as received Him, to them He gave the right to become children of God, to those who believe in His name: who were born, not of blood, nor of the will of the flesh, nor of the will of man, but of God.

John 1:12-13

I can of myself do nothing. As I hear, I judge; and my judgment is righteous, because I do not seek my own will but the will of the Father who sent me.

John 5:30

Whoever receives one of these little children in my name receives me; and whoever receives me, receives not me but him who sent me.

Mark 9:37

But the hour is coming, and now is, when the true worshipers will worship the Father in spirit and truth; for the Father is seeking such to worship Him. God is Spirit, and those who worship Him must worship in spirit and truth.

John 4:23-24

In the spirit and truth of God! This is why:

We walk by faith, not by sight.

2 Corinthians 5:7

And the fundamental basic tool or skill to faith is hearing. Faith comes by hearing—hearing by the word of the Lord. However, faith without good works is dead. Why? Because someone will say, you have faith, and I have works.

Show me your faith without your works, and I will show you my faith by my works.

James 2:18

For in Christ Jesus neither circumcision nor uncircumcision avails anything, but faith working through love.

Galatians 5:6

Because:

For God so loved the world he gave his only begotten Son, that whoever believes in him should not perish but have everlasting life. For God did not send his Son into the world to condemn the world, but that the world through him might be saved.

John 3:16-17

This is the purpose of having *a Savior.* We need to be saved from our petty perverted, divided on everything, polarized, egotistical, hairsplitting, deceitful minded, political church and state of confusion, contradiction of a complex dysfunctional self! *I am Sam,* not a beautiful mind. The fall of man from grace, spiritually retarded, demented, and eternally damned—if it wasn't for God's loving mercy and forgiveness. We are dead meat. Even with the prayers of Jabez, if it ain't son-kissed, it's DOA.

Nevertheless, God loves us—this is God's will. This is what Jesus was all about. God's will is his love. God's love is his law. Almighty God will love you through his law, his will, and this was Jesus's purpose to demonstrate that love through his works, his deeds, the proof of faith working by love. The living testament. ***It is written . . .*** then confessed. This is the gift by and of *God's grace,* the spirit in Jesus. His body is the church, the resurrected Christ, *the head of the church.*

DROP 'N FOR GOD

Pulling into Joe's mobile gas station, I'm on edge. Uneasy. I'm seeing red. Red. Red! It's like an alarm system going off in my head. Red! Red! Warning me that if I feel like this it is the final countdown to an explosion. I am about to erupt. Not with anger but with fear! I feel my greatest fear is about to explode! And that fear is **the Car.** The car is about to do something very expensive because the whole dashboard is lit up! **In red**. This is a **Red Alert!**

I pull into the station and go immediately to the mechanic's service area. I jump out of the car and start yelling, "Hey, Joe. Joe!"

I sound like a circus trooper calling, "Hey, Rube!" "Hey, Rube!" is circus language for **Red Alert,** or help. Hey, Rube! This is a signal that something in wrong. Then all the circus people come a-runnin'. I'm talkin' about midgets, clowns, the fat lady, the lion tamer, elephants—you name it. Here they come. A-runnin'! Hey, Rube! Hey, Rube! Well, that's the way the mechanics came running to my aid. Mobile Harry was leading the charge. Joe, the owner, brought up the rear.

It's like an ambulance rushing into the emergency room on *ER*, or more accurately, it was like an episode of *Scrubs*.

My car was painfully wheeled into the auto bay. Long tentacles stretched from the *diagnostic* computer out and into my vehicle. The computer was interrogating my car, like an MRI scan designed to find all kinds of problems with the body. Oprah got one! Oprah's got everything. She's blessed!

Well, while my car is in the ICU—*intensive care unit*—Joe gets a preliminary printout and studies it intensely. He's got that disturbed look on his face. The look a doctor gets when the news is bad, like "It's terminal! We must operate! You're pregnant, sir!"

Joe clears his throat in a doctorlike fashion, his brow furrows, and his voice has that clinical dread to it—I can feel it. A bad diagnosis is coming! "It don't look good! Alternator, shot! Battery fading. Oil, low down and dirty. Air and oil filters worn and filthy. Tire rotation. Speedometer, DOA."

My mouth dropped, and my face fell like a man fallin' down an elevator shaft. Joe mercifully cushioned the fall when he said, "Mick! I'll make the bill as reasonable as I can. Plus the oil and air filters are on me!" He looked up at me with a small, very small smile on his lips.

However, it wasn't the smile so much as his choice of words and the tone of his voice. He spoke, and I felt comforted. My emotional, stressed-out state of mind seemed to simmer and begin to calm. Suddenly, the world seemed to make sense. Life is beautiful. God bless ya, Tiny Tim!

Leaving Joe's on foot of course, I'm thinking, *This guy Joe, the owner, is a real sweetheart. A beaut! A God-filled man. I can bear witness to that. Joe is a God-filled man, with a godly filling station—that's what!* A genuine smile crossed my face as I headed down the street, thinking how we used to call gas stations *filling stations*.

Fill 'em up, Joe!

That was back in the day—way back when people were a little kinder and less stressed out. Station attendants took pride and joy in giving good customer service. People had a more godly attitude. At least, I saw it that way and felt it too! Being a convert, a child of God, I saw and felt this through a child's innocent eye and mind.

As a child, I could feel God's presence, and I always acknowledged God, giving him my open confessions. Being held in his arms, I always had a warm and safe feeling about life because I always feel the presence of God within. And not to boast, this I believed with all my heart. With all my mind, trusting my feelings in light of my belief. Even as a child, I cherished and respected this feeling of knowing. Knowing God is ever present and will never forsake me. This is a great comfort to my spirit. Even to this day, I am a child of the Most High.

This is what I feel when I go to Joe's gas station—childlike. Because I can feel God's presence. God! The spirit of truth. The spirit I see when I look into Joe's eyes. The tone of truth I hear in the spirit of Joe's voice. When Joe is looking over the itemized problems on the computer printout, they don't sound so threatening.

"Mick! I'll make the bill as reasonable as I can. Plus the oil and air filters are on me!"

I look at Joe, and I thank God. Like God, I trust Joe. Because I know absolutely nothing about cars. Except how to turn 'em on. Drive. Fill 'em up. Oil change. Air for the tires other than that—zilch! I can't even change a tire. I can barely pump the gas. I know nothin', and as for other aspects of my life, that goes as well!

As I walked away, I stopped to look back at our '95 XE Nissan Sentra. It looked happy and white, like the people moving back into Hollywood. The re-gentrificationers.

I turned and crossed the street, laughing with childlike amusement. I realize how fortunate and blessed and secure that is. When you know you're a child of God. A peace bearer. Blessed. A blessing. And Joe was one of my many blessings!

What a good God! This is the conscious thought running foremost through my mind as I start walking west on Franklin Avenue toward the Cahuenga shopping center. I happened to notice one of those check cashing places, where you can cash your check, pay utility bills, wire money, and get money orders. Which reminded me, I need to get a money order for my brother Gene. He needs money. He's a born-again Christian—a new Jew. Gene is currently serving time in a correctional institution in Florida.

I got the money order now. All I need to do is go home, write it up, and mail it . . . and "Be thy brother's keeper" is fulfilled—such is the satisfaction of staying on track with the Lord. He blesses, provides, and increases as your walk grows into his walk . . . more and more each step you take.

I could feel myself glowing from within. I was charged with so much inspiration, I literally felt as if I was floating. My feet were gliding, at times, above the ground. It was *THE* natural high—a pleasant reality that washed over me knowing that he had taken my burden and made light of it. It's like being in a balloon or walking in space. And, with a snap of a finger, I was brought back to earth by a subtle "Yo! Man! Brotha! Let me run dis at ya'!"

Just like that! I'm face-to-face with a man—a black man in his early forties. He's dressed like a street person—a plaid shirt with worn tan khakis. His hair appears to have been relaxed once upon a time, but now it's returning with a vengeance. A return to his Afro roots. Let me tell you, brotha', it will make the return soon if he doesn't get a touch up . . . and quick! He smells of the *streets of Hollywood*. Not unbearable but noticeable. My nose twitches involuntarily.

"Can you help me? Wanna buy this? Ten dollars."

He was holding an unopened box with a Mr. Coffee in it! I could see *Mr. Coffee* through the clear plastic wrapping over the top of the box.

We stood for a moment, as if in a Mexican standoff. Nobody flinched or moved. I broke this hypnotic *nothingness* by reaching for Mr. Coffee. Actually, I took Mr. Coffee out of his hand. Inherently, I realized that the Lord was creating an opportunity to help this man as I accused him, much like a police officer recovering stolen goods by telling him, "You're a liar and a thief!"

The way he reacted physically played out like I punched him in the face. His head recoiled; his eyes rolled back, and then he squinted his eyes, saying, "How you gonna call me a liar and a thief? You don't even know me! Nigga! You wanna buy this or not? Huh?"

Once again, there was the Mexican standoff. This time it was hot and intense but didn't last long. I defused it with a smile, retorting, "You insult me. And deny the truth. And you are a liar *and* a thief!" Then I said, "How much you pay for that? And don't look at the box!" Just to be on the safe side, I placed the top of the box against my chest so his roving eye couldn't check out the price tag visible through the box window.

This was a little puzzling for him. He scratched his head and began to laugh halfheartedly. A nervous laugh coming across like staccato breaths in sync with little eye contact with a swivel head turning this way and that to see who might be watching. Maybe his posse was nearby, at least he was trying to figure out his next move. On the street, it's all about the moves. Backing off, he asks, "You undercover? Huh? You a cop?"

I'm laughing. It's really funny—this whole charade. Entertaining? Yes, but I feel the spirit coming into play. Tongue in cheek, I respond, "Yes! I am a cop!"

His mouth falls open, and he turns to run, but his feet ain't going nowhere. The spirit of God got his trifling butt on hold, an' he ain't goin' nowhere. I stay the course, using my *cop voice*, saying, "A cop for the Lord. And I got yo' lying butt. This is a bust! So! Confess the truth. Get free or bullshit yo'self deeper in yo' hell."

It's something about letting a person come to grips with the true facts about how we can create hell in our own lives—long before we internalize it. Sort of like history repeating itself. *You reap what you sow!* The man/woman dilemma. The fall from grace. Like September 11, 2001, it leaves a bad taste in your mouth. No peace from the human race. It's a divided spiritual *dis*-grace. The anti-Christ; the spirit festering in our inner space.

"So! You'se on patrol? For the Lord? What's yo' assignment?" He made a good and quick comeback. I dropped my head, then smiling slowly, I looked up and said, "Bullshit! Spiritual bullshit! Gotcha! You jive . . . Motha foya!" I stuck, my tongue out. I started laughing.

This seemed to have hit a real funny bone. He broke up and really seemed to be enjoying the moment, then he asked, "Let me get this perfectly clear. You're a cop. For the Lord? And your assignment is . . . bullshit? If you'll pardon my French, that's fucked up. Even for the Lord." He laughed and then abruptly stopped! And just stared at me!

Once again, an awkward moment of stillness develops as we look into one another's eyes to determine what the next move should or would bring. He takes the initiative. "You're serious about your assignment for the Lord, ain't cha? Yeah, I can tell. I can see it in yo' eyes. I hear it in yo' voice. You really know the Lord," he said, pondering.

I knew that he'd found a hook. He was street smart and knew a score when he saw it. The con was on! He smiled slyly and confidently pursued his quest, saying, "And since you know the Lord, you know how the Lord feels about the downtrodden. The hungry an' da' po'. So! I'm all the above. Why not let your heart be on the mercy of the Lord. Help me. My Lord . . . wit' some spare change. Give me som' em, mista' brotha' man!"

He stuck his hand out, grinning like the Cheshire cat from *Alice in Wonderland*. He had a gleam in his eye. He was clever, and he knew by the laws of God, he had me.

Especially, since I confessed and revealed my spiritual identity. He knew I had to obey the law. I had to give him something. If I didn't, I would be more of a hypocrite than him! It's funny how the *unassigned* understand the laws of God in greater depth than the *assigned*. Perhaps this is why Jesus always said to Satan, "**It is written . . .**" This is the principal, or key, to "We all fall short of his glory." Can't read? That's why faith comes by hearing—"I heard that!"

I really began to see this man, his conning smile as he piled on the streetwise bull jive, but the real man—the soul brother—was in his eyes. There, I saw the spiritual reflection of his soul. The sincerity of a hurting soul. A soul crying out for help. And this is the assignment: *To be an uplifter, a ray of hope, a voice in the wilderness of the darkness of the lost, the fallen, the doubtful, and wavering.* Even for those with *no faith*—yet to be awakened. That's the other side of the coin . . . to gently awaken his soul to his purpose so that he could find remedy for his plight. To be the light, so to speak, as a representative of God. Standing in the gap for God, I spoke, "God's mercy, forgiveness, and understanding be with you. God cherishes those God loves. And your God wants you to know, He loves you. But! God ain't accepting your lying, backslidin', thieving bullshit. Okay? Go, the Creator is not to be mocked!

As I started to walk away, I could see out of the corner of my eye he still had his hand out. I stopped, sucked in a mouth full of air, and blew it out. Slowly, I turned; and as I did, I could see and feel his humbled spirit. Yet! Renewed faith—and faith is revealed from faith to faith—my heart was touched. I walked back to him. With much love, I reached into my pocket and gave tithes to the *church*. My spiritual decree was plain and simple, and I spoke to him directly and to the point, saying, "By the way, God's about transformation. Being born-again. A new creature. Your internal change. And eternal life. Here! Take this and repent. God don't like thieves and liars."

I handed him five dollars and gave him back Mr. Coffee. I turned and walked north on Wilcox. As I make the turn, he yells out after me, "Yo', brotha! Thank you! And much praise. To God! You got yo' God thing down. Stay up! You drop 'n knowledge and change 4 God!"

THY BROTHER OF CHRIST!

Thy brother of Christ . . . to the brethren who of spirit is pure and totally committed to the doing of our Father's will and to the *brotherhood of Christ.*

To the voice of John the Baptist who as a *masterful messenger* of the Almighty Master, a royal son in the body of Christ for Jews and Gentiles alike, whose still, silent reminder is heard amongst the believers, crying, "Cry on! Cry out! Cry out for joy! Cry, baby, cry!"

But as you so joyously cry, never forget you're not alone and never, never have you been forsaken! Because God, *Our Father,* has your back, and we have his word. He never will abandon you! So *cry on!*

Like Jesus, you've got to wake up **LAZARUS, THE INNER CITY.** And when you wake up these sleeping giants for Christ, you'll see the brilliance of our real soldiers come forth in brotherhood and love. For love is the fulfillment of the law. God's eternal love and mercy for the lost. Especially those lost in *da' ghetto.* This caused Jesus to say, "Get my lost . . ."

For these are some of the lost descendants of Abraham—the father of the faithful and the just, who justly live by faith. Not church and state where Satan poli-tricks world religion! Under the new covenant with Jesus, the word, the son, the resurrected spirit of God, *Our Father,* is made manifest and stands with you.

There's the *ghetto sheep*—lost and gone astray from the center of the fold—from *Our Father.* They have forgotten their greatest gift, the only way to freedom—*LOVE. It is written* . . . love is the fulfillment of the law. God's will be done. *Love ye one another as I love ye!* Love your God.

Love your neighbor, *and always* love your enemy!

And those who love like this and place their faith by the law, believing the love of the law, they will be found just. They are the faithful. For the just live by faith and love it. This is the condition of love and not that of the *un!*

So my faithful lover of the truth and the just, *cry on!* Let the spirit of the word in you be heard. Speak on the word! And stand boldly on God's word.

Those with ears will hear, and when the trumpet sounds, the hearers will appear near and very dear. You are family in the body of Christ—Jews and Gentiles alike! All will hear the joyous singing of *"Oh come all ye faithful . . ."*

It is written . . . there is no defense against God's love! God's love, the divine conditional law for the human spirit. The foundation of Christ and his kingdom, heaven here on earth. One nation! One God! One family! One love!

God bless you my dear, precious, and so dedicated darling brothers in the body of Christ.

With all love, your brother,

Mick E.

HEY, MAN!

" **H**ey, *Man.*" In fact, Mr. Man, you're quite a man! A good man. A man in da' process of becoming a Man—a state called *Man-hood*. Hu-**man**-i-ty. A MAN passing through da' hood—**boy**-hood.

One of the essential principles of childhood, which includes either/or the combined whole of childhood. Children. A boy or a girl. Wo-**man**-hood. Childhood, boy or girl, male or female, gay or straight, wo-man—all **is** man-kind. This is the combination that makes the flavor of Da' Hood cool and alive. The life we perceive as our hood—our covering, our foreskin—the self-hood, the ego-hood, is the reason why the *hood* is misunderstood. It's like Marvin said, "What's goin' on?"

In all the *Hood of Rap*, it's elegantly stated, "What's up? It's all in da' mix. Who's life is it? Serious questions. Life of ownership. Man, you're movin' about in the life—a gift from God. It's not ours to give or to take or to own."

Yet most folks take life totally out of perspective with one statement: "This is my life! I do what and with it as I please. It's my life." And life for the most part is a mixture of double standards. Yours versus everybody else. Including God's. Allah, Jehovah, Jesus whoever!

Let's see what the dictionary says "life" is, my man. **Hey, Man!** Yeah **you!**

LIFE: The quality that distinguishes a vital and functional being from a *dead body.*

The sequence of physical and mental experiences that make up the existence of an individual.

The period from birth to death.

Now let's see what the biblical reference to life reveals. Life starts with God, the author and inspiration of the creation for life. In the inspired Scripture, *It is written . . .*

In the beginning God created the heavens and the earth.

Genesis 1:1

And the Lord God formed man of the dust of the ground, and breathed into his nostrils the breath of life; and man became a living being.

Genesis 2:7

That's why breathing is so essential and vital to life. Without *the breath of life* there can be no life. Yet we all live and die. We live as long as we breathe. We die when we stop breathing. One way or the other. The circumstances or details of the cause of death, the loss of breath, may vary. Details change, the principle remains the same. Without breath, you're dead! Now! That's some bad breathe. None! Zero—dead, death waiting to exhale.

Even though we experience death, God our Creator, Lord, and Father is merciful and has given us the resurrected redemption from death. In the resurrected life of his only begotten son **Christ Jesus,** who is life himself. The very image of man, and he bought back our sovereignty because he conquered death for man. Those whosoever truly believe and trust in him shall be saved. Saved for eternal life. Praise God by always giving God the glory. For God gave us the ultimate gift: **LIFE** *eternal!*

For when we seek the kingdom of God first in all things, God will send forth his Holy Spirit, filled with wisdom, to guide and help us understand his kingdom on earth.

> *Does not wisdom cry out and understanding lift up her voice? Listen, for I will speak of excellent things. And from the opening of my lips will come right things. For my mouth will speak truth. Wickedness is an abomination to my lips. All the words of my mouth are with righteousness. Nothing crooked or*

perverse is in them. They are all plain to him who understands and right to those who find knowledge.

Receive my instructions and not silver, and knowledge rather than choice gold.

For wisdom is better than rubies and all the things one may desire cannot be compared with her wisdom.

Now, therefore, listen to me my children, hear instructions and be wise. For whoever finds me finds life. And, obtains favor from the Lord.

(excerpts of Proverbs 8 and Psalms 119)

This is life. A grace-filled gift from God, *Our Father,* who loves us and seeks to enlighten us. We are of the seed of Abraham, for **It is written . . .** that God spoke to Abraham and said that from his seed will come many nations—to form the new nation of one family, one human family—Jews and Gentiles alike. God's will is goodwill toward man and his kind. **Hey, Man . . .** A-men!

Life is not lived by faith alone but also by the good deeds done in his name. The dynamic duo of **faith and good works** is better by far than Starsky and Hutch or Cheech and Chong! This is how you will truly know people who care for God—by their deeds performed in faith in the one true God, *Our Father.* Not the will of their lifestyles or sexual preferences, their selfish or egotistically politically correct spirit of the author of world religion. Church of sad state. The *me-first* attitude born of being deluded into believing the original liar and deceiver himself! Satan! Who is the author of *no peace, no justice, no truth, no trust, and no love.* Just ex-rated, ex-file, ex-treme, ex-terminate. This is why shit happens. Freaks! They're everywhere *ha, ha, ha.* Not funny! X it! Stage left snaggle puss!

It is the sincere hope of *Our Father* that you enjoy the experiences of life and delight in them. But *know* we are not **of** this earth, rather travelers **in** it, walking not by sight but by faith! So take what you see with a grain of salt. Salt with no flavor might as well be thrown out; it is dead! Life lived to the fullest in the grace and love of ***Christ Jesus*** is a good life. For he stands one with**in** you. Turning your back on this promise renders you dead to him who loves you and a slave to him who despises you. You will know no peace and have nothing but trouble wherever you turn until you return to *Our Father,* God Almighty, who always waits on his *prodigal son* to return. Not all that glitters is gold, and beauty is not in the sight but in the soul.

Know first the kingdom of God, and all else will be added. But understand that it's a package deal when you enter into a personal relationship with God 'n da' body of Christ. Faith and good works—the fulfillment of the law. ***LOVE!*** *It is written . . .*

> *Man shall not live by bread alone but by every word that proceeds from the mouth of God.*
>
> Matthew 4:4

Hey, Man. I love writing like this.

CHILDREN . . . THE HERITAGE OF GOD'S LOVE

A Child: An unborn or recently born person. A young person. Especially between infancy and youth.

Children: More than one child.

We are a child of the flesh. A biological child of earthly parents or guardians, and we are the child of God in the body of Christ. But first, the child must be **born again** to a spiritual connection to our Creator and Redeemer. You can't be both, without being born twice . . . and dying once. *Hmm.*

Why does God place so much emphasis on children? Mainly because children are the foundation and starting point for the kingdom of heaven—here on earth.

And let's see what Scripture says about God's commandments, laws, and his love for children. God began with instructions for parents and the society:

> *Train up a child in the way he or she should go, and when he is old he will not depart from it.*
>
> Proverbs 22:6

And do children, trained or not trained, give children the right to be excused from doing wrong things or being disobedient? And does God overlook these wrong doings, whether intentional or unintentional?

According to Scripture:

> *Even a child is known by his or her deeds, whether what he does is pure and right.*
>
> Proverbs 20:11

In the Book of Mark 9:36, "Jesus spoke to his twelve disciples by example. He took a child and set him on his lap as he sat in the midst of them. After he had done this, he said,"

> *Whoever receives one of these little children in my name receives me; and whoever receives me, receives not me, but him who sent me.*
>
> Mark 9:37

This makes it clear for a believer raised and trained to be a true follower of Christ that children are our blessings. A gift from God.

> *Let the little children come to me, and do not forbid them; for of such is the kingdom of God. Assuredly, I say to you, whoever does not receive the kingdom of God as a little child will by no means enter it.*
>
> Mark 10:14-15

> *Behold, children are a heritage from the Lord, the fruit of the womb is a reward.*
>
> Psalm 127:3

Heritage: Property that descends *(comes down)* to an heir.

So if children are a heritage from the Lord and comes through the womb of a woman and into the body of Christ, then the child is a reward to the believer. But the fruit, *a.k.a.* **the child** belongs to God. And the child inherently knows this because the child is a heritage of the Lord. Since we all fall short of the glory of God, the child needs to be made aware of the relationship of *Our Father*. God is royal, beyond word, therefore the child in youth must be encouraged to develop devotion for his *divine Father* and establish his loyalty to God, first and foremost.

Who is the greatest in the kingdom of heaven? This was a question the disciples posed to Jesus. Jesus called a little child to him and, placing the child in the midst of them, said,

> *Assuredly, I say to you, unless you are converted and become as little children, you will by no means enter the kingdom of heaven. Therefore whoever humbles himself as this little child is the greatest in the kingdom of heaven. Whoever receives one little children like this in my name receives me.*
>
> Matthew 18:3-5

> *But as many as received him, to them he gave the right to become children of God, to those who believe in his name: who were born, not of blood, nor of the will of the flesh, nor of the will of man, but of God.*
>
> John 1:12-13

So, young people, take not this time of your youth and childhood lightly. For it is your sincerity and belief in God's only begotten son that gives you strength and reality to your faith.

Faith is a daily practice of a conscious effort. Through prayer and meditating on God's words, in searching the Scriptures and being open to his divine revelation. It's seeking ye first the kingdom of God and all his righteousness. Asking God and receiving. Knocking on the door of the spirit and having it open.

Reading the Bible is wonderful. Quoting Scripture is a delight. But you will be known by your deeds. And your faith in God. Because,

ACTIONS SPEAK LOUDER THAN WORDS!

And it's your committed action, framed in faith in he who sent his son to be crucified for the redemption of sin, that allows the holy spirit of Christ, the church, the light of the world, to be a lamp unto your feet.

AMEN!

TO DA MAN: THE DUDE

Hip! Hip! Hurrah! Hip Hop! And don't you dare stop.
"Congratulations to Our Son"
With vicarious pleasure, it is indeed a privilege,
A most congenial honor to present to you:

Mr. Toren Michael Jones

This plaque of love and deepest respect to this moment
Of your High School accomplishment to:
GRADUATE
You ran the course while setting your own pace
And now you have completed the race.
It's not about first, second, or last.
Neither is it about the grades you did or did not pass.
No! It's about the start and the finish.
To complete the race with human dignity and grace.

Toren, you have achieved the distinction of "A Graduate"
And received as proof, a Certificate,
"A Degreed Diploma" of meritorious valor.
In recognition of your dedicated effort and success
In surviving birth, childhood, and the
Treacherous teenage transitional psychological steps to
"Adulthood." Basically, the effects of "Parenthood"
Now! This plaque is your reward, a symbol of your dues
Of growing pains paid in full: "U-N-Da' Hood"

Toren, you have "hoodwinked" and cleverly acquired Life
Skills.
You have honed your "International Intellectual Awareness"
*To an artistic hue of brilliant **"Ideals."***
And, you have charted the course of your Destiny
With a strong and unbending Will.

And, finally, you are about to embark on a journey
To travel on the horizon only YOU can chart.

So, My Man, Sail On!

Once again, Congratulations!
*From a **God** who **cares about You.***
It's a personal thang!
Peace . . . out! Mom & Dad

The "Call!"

As I write this piece, "The 'Call!'" I'm very amused with myself. Because, "The 'Call!'" was inspired by a phone conversation I had with Uncle Johnny—my father's younger brother. It was I who called him.

Uncle Johnny and I have enjoyed some very in-depth, deep conversations. Our relationship could be considered an *afflicted* relationship. Because it has always been based on conflict, contradiction, and straight-up verbal confrontation of the zaniest and wackiest sort.

Our relationship with all of its affliction is at the core of our love for one another. Now this long-standing foundation being shaken by *O*-pinion-ation. This is what brings me to the table, pen in hand and paper ready.

I write with reflection on our early relationship. A farce, like most marriages, which is what a relationship really is, technically speaking. A marriage is a bond, a relationship, one in which bonding is supposed to take place. And Uncle Johnny and I are bonded. A dangerous marriage—as Bond, James Bond, is married to danger. Yes, our relationship is double *O*-pinion-ated. Da' cold finga! But tonight, well, we experienced something totally off the radar. We flipped each other off!

As early as I can remember, Uncle "OO Honey" Johnny and our cold finga' relationship began when I was told to call him Uncle Johnny. Mainly because my mother and father kept saying, "This is Uncle Johnny." So I called him Uncle Johnny, and he began calling me smart guy. He'd say, "You're a smart guy, aren't you?" And I'd say, "You got that right!"

Uncle Johnny would laugh his cackling laugh. His eyes squinting, veins popping out of his temple, he'd shake his head, speechless, then say, "Boy, with knowledge like that already in your head, you can make somebody hurt you. 'Cause you're talkin' way beyond a kid. You're talkin' like somebody grown. In fact, you're talkin' better than grown people. Just wait till you grow up."

And I'd just stare at him. Then, I'd say, "Why do they call you Uncle Johnny?"

He'd say, "See, you're not as smart as you think you are."

And I'd say, "That's because I'm kid talkin' grown. So why are you my uncle?

Then Uncle Johnny would say, "I've got something for you, smart guy. See if you can repeat this:

Lil' Fly on the wall
Ain't you got no clothes at t'all?
Ain't you got no fancy slip?
Ain't you got no pants to zip?
Awe lil' Fly.

Not only did I repeat it, I added another line to it. I repeated the whole thing, and when I got to the part about "ain't you got no pants to zip," I added, "You ain't even got no wine to sip. Awe lil' Fly. Whack!"

Then Uncle Johnny would laugh, shake his head, but at the same time, he'd look a little distraught and would say, "What kind of a kid are you that would mess up a Paul Lawrence Dunbar's classic poem with a murder. What do you have to say for yourself?"

And I would just look at him with childlike *knowing*, saying, "The fly wasn't going nowhere. He has a short attention span, low self-esteem, and no ID."

Then Uncle Johnny would laugh in that exasperated adult desperation way. After getting himself back together again, he'd try one of his cleverest little spills. He always felt I was smart, but that he was more clever. After all, he was the oldest and had lived the longest. Like Oscar Brown Jr. cutting a fast rip on one of his social commentary and poetic pieces, Uncle Johnny would scat, like *All That Jazz*.

> *Who dat! Say, Who Dat!*
> *When I say, Who Dat!*
> *Now, who said Dat!*
> *Who Dat!*

I'd just look at Uncle Johnny like a child looking at a toy he doesn't understand but is very amused by it. I'd smile to myself—that all-knowing smile only children have when they know they know—but just don't know why they know what they know. Yet they know they know! Know what I mean?

At this point, Uncle Johnny interrupted my interphasing on the reflection of the revelation I'd just accepted within myself as the truth, saying, "Ah huh! Gotcha, didn't I? You ain't so smart on that WHO DAT, are you?"

We kept talkin'. There was great silence, warmth, joy, and triumph coming over me. It was as if a giant wave was about to engulf me with great anticipation. It was a back to the womb feeling. Knowing som'em even before you come out into the gotcha.com world. You kinda know where you're going. *Praise God.*

Now Uncle Johnny is pressing me to come up with something, saying, "Come on, smart guy. What do you got to say?"

I looked at him straight in the eye, and with love, I said, "Why are you my uncle?"

Now as I sit here with pen in hand, I laugh and am truly amused while at the same time feeling remorse. Why? Because Uncle Johnny and I had just had one of our conflicts, contradictions, confrontations, wicky wacky telephone conversations—a conversation which I initiated. I had called him! *Oh God, why?*

After hanging up the phone, I sit here contemplating what had just "expired," and I say "expired" because as I hung up, I felt the relationship had just died. It's like *the call* was death. *Double-O-Cold Fingah!*

The call wasn't cold--it was dead! ***Dead cold!***

Yes, for the first time, it was just not there—deceased.

Death had crept in from its crypt and shaken the foundation of our relationship. Our bond. Our marriage was devastated by a very cock-eyed *O-pinion*. Our bullshit marriage was now in shambles. Nonsense! For the first time, we made *no sense*. That is good sense for expanding our understanding and our knowledge. However, God said, "Lean not on your own understanding."

Maybe that was the problem. We knew too much. Yet like everyone else, we knew nothing. With all of our knowledge, we knew no thing! **In the Moment,** I realized I had taken God's understanding and God's wisdom of that knowledge and became the adversary: *Satan*. **Oops, dere it iz!**

Like Satan, I became angry and became self-righteous in **my** understanding. I became like the letter of the law. Legalistic to the max. For I ended the conversation and almost disconnected a long-standing relationship—biological and very spiritual.

So in this moment of self-righteousness, God spoke and chastised me, and I cried out in confession and shame! Repenting, "Thank you, true God of the living, please fo'give me!

So let's all enjoy the forgiveness. Whatever the ups and downs, lumps and bumps, difference and/or indifference, conflict, contradictions, confrontations, AND *O-pinionations*. Call it all **JOY**. Because this is what counts. God's word establishes good will. As it was in the beginning, it is now and forever more; *nevertheless*, God the true and living God is the *best* . . . and does more than bless.

So seek!

Ask!

And knock!

And, you will find you kno'.

And, Gabrielle will blow.

And, Peter will open da' do'e.

And, in heaven you'll see Christ.

Da' Divine. His Milk and Honey

Da' flo.

Now after all that sincere confession, repenting, and lamenting, I'm glad I made *The CALL!*

I love you, Uncle Johnny, *Double O Honey.*

Rest in peace . . .

A PHONE COUGH!

Ah! What a good morning! A most refreshing, restful, harmonious, peaceful good morning. This *"Good Morning"* God has blessed as a morning filled with good. It's already bubbling and brimming like a good cup of coffee.

Yet steams like tea and smells a bit like hot cocoa . . . even a cup of Ovaltine. This *is* a good morning—an instant, *all*-right morning. And all I have done so far is open my eyes. *Darn!* God is good!

God is so good, as a matter-of-fact, that I didn't even say *damn.* This morning is too good to damn 'cause as you think, so you are! That's a proverb, I believe.

Man, I'm feeling so darn good, and I know where this good feeling is coming from. It's from the divine cup of *spiritual harmony* sweetened with *mutual oneness* . . . and may I add, it is overflowing!

A spillover of the delight and reflection of last night—a night of pure joy! And all in the spirit of love. This was the spirit I felt and was in the very moment I opened my eyes. I was like LTD—**bam!** Back in love again. Because I was still engulfed by God's anointing and spiritual enchantment.

Last night! Now the morning after! The morning after a great revelation of God's continuity of presence. His never forsaking, never abandoning, and always gifting those who turn their hearts toward him. All of these thoughts, feelings, and insights were being showered on me this blessed morning as I recalled the wonderful and gifted people I'd been with at the *wrap party*. A party—crew, staff, joining cast, mingled with the producer and director in celebration of the creation of an independent *Joe Cole* film entitled **Shadow Boxing**. This film was created with love, artistic ardor, and with a high-profile zeal. It was an inexpensive production with a major league look. Wrapped, completed, and finished! *That's all, folks!* Except postproduction, it was o'va!

Over, except for the feeling I had this morning, for it was exactly like how I'd felt last night. I keep going back to that feeling. A feeling that went much deeper than I realized . . . until now!

Aha! *N*ow it dawns on me! I'm being spiritually assailed with my hammer of love to the heart, opening my *heart of remembrance* with the memory of a very warm, loving, divine spiritual experience. We were just a bunch of tech people, actors, and filmmakers who were driven by more than the usual commercial obsessions. *We had* **compassion!**

Not the usual attitude you find in the film industry. No! This group radiated love! A caring and unselfish sharing spirit. It was something to observe and spiritually be engulfed in. The only odd thing about this wrap party was that I don't remember hearing any *rap music,* which brings me back to my feeling so good on this *very* good morning!

While wrapped in a cocoon of spiritual warmth tethered to last night's party, my phone rings, and I can feel the sealing wax beginning to melt. It was a phone call boiling over with *attitude.* It was THE *coughing* phone call.

As the phone rang, I picked it up, saying with my usual morning candor, "Good morning, Mick E. Jones at your service."

I stand there with my cordless phone snuggled into my left ear, which, by the way, reminded me to take my LEFT FOOT back to blockbuster; but in any event, I wait, phone pressed against my left ear, for a word or two from the person on the other end. Without warning, suddenly there it is—***a lot of coughing!*** I say it again, a lot of coughing—not just a clearing of the throat or dislodging of something or another. I mean coughing, the kind you hear in the TB wards of county hospitals!

It was a hard cough. Deep and penetrating with a gagging aftermath. It sounded as if someone was having a really ***serious*** moment with themselves. Out of concern, I said to the caller, "Hello? Hello, you okay?"

The coughing continued. I rubbed my forehead, trying to figure out what's going on! I heave a heavy sigh and cordially inquire, "Excuse me, you okay?"

Still nothing—just dead air. I was about to say "have a good day" when I heard this crass, gruff, scratchy, throaty voice speak, saying, "Do I sound the fuck okay?" Then and there, my mind went on *pause*. Spitting it out, he wretches into the phone, saying, "Well, whatcha' gonna say to that motha'fucka'?" During this brief verbal interlude, he was coughing, expectorating, and cussing. Immediately, I have a knee-jerk reaction to hang up. *Slam!* But instead I ask, "Did you cover your mouth?"

This act of goodwill and humane kindness seemed to amuse the caller—*Mr. Crass Throat/Crude Rudy/The Voice*. Forgive me if I call a spade a spade, however, with street shit written into his voice, he coughed violently, then remarked with dark, cutting-edge rudeness, "Why da' fuck should I cover my mouth? I'm talking to yo' ass, dude!"

This was a real testy reality check to my faith because I didn't want to abandon the blessings that this very good morning had brought upon me. I could hear the voice of my faith calmly saying, "Let not the circumstances dictate your faith."

Besides, I know *Crude Rudy* ain't talking to my ass, like he said, "I know where I got the phone." Nevertheless, I realize this has to be addressed, undressed, then redressed 'cause God's people ain't to be mocked!

Politely, having the patience of Job, with the voice of understanding and wisdom, using my God-given sound mind and authority, I spoke correctively and with kindness and love, "When you're having a coughing seizure in someone's ear, it's in good taste and common manners to say 'excuse me!'"

No matter the source of my intentions, be they well meaning, good manners, good taste, or common sense, or not, all it got me was more coughing. With rejuvenated purpose and sickly pride, *Mr. Crass/Crude Rudy* began coughing and gagging nastier and more disgustingly than before, stopping only to quiz me with, "How cha' like dat? How was it? What's yo' take on that, motha' fucka'? Got a Scripture for that?"

I responded in a very low-key and laid-back way. I said, "Personally, I didn't like it. How was it? Like you! Gross, ill-mannered, sad, sick, angry, and spiritually retarded. My take on this thus far? You should take a nap! Now some Scriptures for you."

> *Therefore, as the elect of God, holy and beloved, put on tender mercies, kindness, humility, meekness, longsuffering; bearing with one another, and forgiving one another, if anyone has a complaint against another; even as Christ forgave you, so you also must do.*
>
> Colossians 3:12-13

Countering with what seemed his best coughing, gagging, hacking, yelling routine to date, which apparently he'd developed into a negative *art form*, he sputtered on with great pride and boastful hostility, "How you like dat, motha'fucka'? How's that make your script-quoting day? Asshole! Because this really makes my motha'fuckin' day."

Coughing violently, he spat out other unpleasant deletes, then hung up; and just like that, it was over!

Gently, I placed the phone back into its cradle. Then I reached for the CD remote, clicked on AWB, got an O'Doul's green, and sat down at the dining room table. I pulled over my legal pad, picked up my friend *da' pen,* and thanked God for another good day . . . and **It was written . . .**

The moral to the story: As it was in the beginning with God, it will be in the end. GOOD MORNING, and it still is!

Okay? *Snap!*

Heed "The Children"

We, as a world society of adults, educators, parents, and people in general, need to rethink the value of children. Especially those calling themselves *spiritual leaders*. Because many of the attitudes, biases, and perceptions are rooted, then nurtured in early childhood.

Children and the stage of life we refer to as *childhood* are taken much to lightly by far too many. Specifically, children's abilities to articulate and express the environmental experiences they are witness to, as well as participants in, is a direct responsibility of the parent. The burden of being a parent is awesome. Showing another to the way of understanding and using this flood of emotional and psychological input is staggering. To apprehend, comprehend, and integrate all of this sensory, intellectual, and emotional information requires total commitment and willingness to step up to the plate of social consciousness.

This childhood process that formulates the outlook of the adult, whether it is negative, positive, good, evil, right, or wrong is the foundation of our society. The natural instinctive learning process of children has always been in delicate balance with the psychic. Instinct is everything.

The supreme spirit has given great indication by spiritual inspiration, channeled through believers, about the power of children. For the child is the foundation of the next adult. All folks start and develop by the cause and the effects of early childhood.

Childhood, the building or stumbling block of humanity—*war or peace!*

> *The wolf also shall dwell with the lamb, The leopard shall lie down with the young goat, The calf and the young lion and the fatling together; and a little child shall lead them.*
>
> Isaiah 11:6

> *Let the little children come to me, and do not forbid them; for of such is the kingdom of heaven.*
>
> Matthew 19:14

> *Train up a child in the way he should go, and when he is old he will not depart from it.*
>
> Proverbs 22:6

Parents in general have been educated (institutional brainwashing) out of their biological capacity to trust their instincts. The natural intelligence of *good sense*. The natural logic or the ability to understand and make practical and applicable sense out of common reasoning for the good of the human race.

The obvious objective of the spirit within—the spiritual objective education can never teach, and government institutions willfully destroy, is called **PEACE**. *The inner peace of God.*

This is why the average adult, who is a victim of this institutionally taught deficiency, can't or won't accept *the truth* as heard through the peaceful, intuitive, analytical skills of a child. The adult inner ear—*the spirit ear*—has been deafened by the noise of a world bent on its own decimation. Children, while still a child, have the ability to decipher and identify this negativity, which society throws upon them. Their spirit within has the innate ability to identify it. Thus, they rebel and repel or conform, but still raise hell!

Children are a barometer for a society that fails them. And consequently, they fall into the GAP. Like father, like son. The apple never falls far from the tree. They repeat the same errors of their parents. They underestimate a child's insight. A gift from God.

God, for those who sincerely believe there is a God and not the religious or politically correct god of government, but rather God, the universal Almighty God! *Our Father,* the Lord, has inspired a psalmist to say,

Behold children are a heritage from the Lord, . . .

Psalm 127:3

So save the children and save the world! This is the good will of God toward the world. *Peace*. A childhood necessity. The spirit within and children are the primary barometer of God's will. **Peace.**

> *Blessed are the peacemakers, for they shall be called sons of God.*
>
> Matthew 5:9

A Request Addressed

Hello and greetings! In the name of Jesus, the resurrected Christ. The holy matrimony of spirit to spirit.

Our spiritual marriage to the Holy Spirit, now the body of Christ Jesus, the living church, the glory of God, a confession for the true believers has given rise to the nature of our relationship with God, *Our Father,* and the *institution* of marriage. First and foremost, marriage is a holy union with God. Second to that is the union of man and woman. However, let it be said, "What God has put together, let no man put asunder" is a worthy admonition. For without God at the core of the union, the marriage is nothing more than a sham, even though the imprint of love may have been the abiding factor in saying, "I do!" In the end, it will be lust, not love, that dominates the marriage.

So I have searched the Scriptures in order to further identify factors at play in our need to understand what makes up the state of being married. According to Scripture,

All Scripture is given by inspiration of God, and is profitable for doctrine, for reproof, for correction, for instruction in righteousness.

2 Timothy 3:16

The "state of being married" is defined academically as:

The mutual relationship of husband and wife. Wedlock. The institution whereby men and women are joined in a special kind of social and legal dependency for the purpose of founding and maintaining a family or dysfunctional world government.

Merriam Webster's Collegiate Dictionary/Mick E.

Married to the bridegroom—Jesus. Giving birth to family—unity. This is the circle of Eternal Life. Born again—free. To love ye one another.

Now! "**Marriage**" is defined in **the Bible**, New King James Version, in a number of passages. I will start with 1 Corinthians, chapter 7.

In this section, the Apostle Paul is speaking to the Corinthians in Corinth. At the time, the most important city in Greece. Corinth was a bustling hub of worldwide commerce, degraded culture and idolatrous religion (like Vegas and Hollywood). Paul was addressing all of this, as well as marriage. Here are some principles of marriage:

Now concerning the things of which you wrote to me: It is good for a man not to touch a woman. Nevertheless, because of sexual immorality, let each man have his own wife, and let each woman have her own husband. Let the husband render to his wife the affection due her, and likewise also the wife to her husband. The wife does not have authority over her own body, but the husband does. And likewise the husband does not have authority over his own body, but the wife does. Do not deprive one another except with consent for a time, that you may give yourselves to fasting and prayer; and come together again so that Satan does not tempt you because of your lack of self-control."

1 Corinthians 7:1-5

But I say to the unmarried and to the widows: It is good for them if they remain even as I am; but if they cannot exercise self-control, let them marry. For it is better to marry than to burn with passion.

1 Corinthians 7:8-9

Marriage is honorable among all, and the bed undefiled; but fornicators and adulterers God will judge.

Hebrews 13:4

Regarding marriage, as it applies to the Church and Christ:

Wives, submit to your own husbands, as to the Lord.

For the husband is the head of the wife, as also Christ is the head of the church; and he is the Savior of the body.

Therefore, just as a church is subject to Christ, so let the wives be to their own husbands in everything.

Husbands, love your wives, just as Christ also loved the church and gave Himself for her, that he might sanctify and cleanse her with the washing of water by the word, that he might present her to himself a glorious church, not having spot or wrinkle or any such thing, but that she should be holy and without blemish.

So husbands ought to love their own wives as their own bodies; he who loves his wife loves himself.

For no one ever hated his own flesh, but nourishes and cherishes it, just as the Lord does the church. For we are members of his body, of his flesh and of his bones.

For this reason a man shall leave his father and mother and be joined to his wife, and the two shall become one flesh.

This is the great mystery, but I speak concerning
Christ and the church.

Nevertheless let each one of you in particular so love
his own wife as himself, and let the wife see that she
respects her husband.

Ephesians 5:22-33

I hope these findings by Scripture have enlightened your faith as *we walk by faith not by sight*. The law of God's will is love! **Not** lust.

SHAKE IT UP, BABY!

Shake it up, baby! I'm twistin', exhileratin', and vibratin'! I'm **ALL SHOOK UP!** Um-humm . . .

I tell y'all, I feel better than Saturday night fever, or *Sunday morning boogalooin'* down a church aisle shoutin', "**I FEEL GOOD!**"

By the way, I'm in the Book of James—James Brown, that is—and he says, "Hey! Shake it up, baby! Burp! And gurp! A child is born. Long live da' queen!"

Yeah! That's what this exhilarating, joyful moment is all about! The joyous excitement of birth. An exceedingly great exhortation as when **A CHILD IS BORN.** For when a child is born, it always represents hope—to be *born again*—alive, filled with promise. The living testament of *Our Father*: child birth.

Just think, every time a child is born, the parents have been given the privilege, the pleasure, and the honorable opportunity to bring into the world a disciple, a peace bearer for the living God!

But if the child doesn't know or have a personal relationship with the true and living God, God help us! And if the children don't believe in God, *good golly, Miss Molly,* it's Rosemary's baby. *Children of the Damned!* Every day, *Friday the 13th!*

Childhood is then just another scary movie . . . unless the parents have that higher consciousness of a supreme spirit, the spirit we know to be God, *Our Father.* And that is the spirit and pontificating mode I'm excited by and in. Why? Because I have been notified that a child is born—**again!**

And it is the notification of this great divine event that has triggered off these celebratory written declarations of great joy and well-wishes of spiritual congratulations. *Happy Mother's Day—and Father's too!*

This was all prompted by a recent letter that I received from a former student of a boxing class I instruct at the Hollywood YMCA. For the record, Angie, but I call her *Angel* because she has an angelic smile and spirit. She's strong in spirit, a survivor, a giver, and a seeker of truth. An earth angel. *Have mercy, Mr. Percy!*

The seeking of truth is where Angel's real strength and courage lay. This is why confession is good for the soul. Yet as we must come to God in spirit and truth, so Angel's confessions are always clear, truthful, and right to the point.

Angel's first confession was she had recently had a beautiful baby girl. Her name is Helene (pronounced L-N, stressing the *N*).

Then Angel confessed that she and her live-in loved one, Chris, hadn't planned on having that beautiful baby until they got married. But unfortunately, the baby didn't know that. **Oops, dere it iz!** Ain't that a b—, baby out of wedlock 4-U. *Whazz up, Doc?*

The next confession was even better than that one. When she got pregnant, she got scared. I said to myself as I read that confession, "Damn! Why do people get scared after the fact? If you ain't scared to be live-ins and lov'n in da' bed, when the unplanned baby comes, why get scared? 'Cause you ain't wed? Ain't cha' still in love? Why is doubt running through yo' head? Peekaboo, God is still with you."

I'm really starting to enjoy these true confessions. Priests don't get it this good. They have to go through too many Hail Marys.

As I read on regarding some of the other confessed fears, besides not planning for parenthood—a dual purpose for a single function—was the fear of not enough money. And they didn't know themselves well enough to start a family. Unfortunately, the baby wasn't up on this part. The baby only could do its part by being born.

Now the baby—*Lady Helene*—is born. Born without the slightest clue as to any plans for her manifestation, the baby listens to God as the parents anguish. They declare they have no money but are in love, unwed, and not sure that they really know themselves. But the fact they believe they are in love is the saving grace, thank God!

These confessions continue to get better as Angel confessed more: "The natural question for us [which everyone else is asking] is about marriage."

"I know you, and I've talked about this before. The only thing holding me back is fear," as Angel's words seem to *cry out!* That crying out has got me really thinking. She (they) weren't afraid to be a *live-in.* Not afraid to have a baby, unwed, scarce finance, and lack of in-depth knowledge of the foundation of a relationship, the backbone of parenthood, yet saying "*I Do*" or "*We Do*" brings the ring of fear.

And these fears have a lot of variations according to these delightful and wonderful confessional dilemmas. Angel fears not living her life the way everyone she grew up with does or, at least, expects her to.

I believe Angel got that measure of fear backward. I believe this fear of not *living life the way others do* is invalid. But it's the fear of becoming what they appear to have become: *dysfunctional, divorced, and deranged.* Now dats da' norm! Scary, *huh?*

It's that fear that has alienated them from a religious ceremonial wedding of the Catholic flavor—or any blend of a church ritual. A paper, a legal document of marriage, because she's seen so much hypocrisy. This scares Angel. On that scene, she dislikes going to church. The experience left a bitter taste in her mouth. Mostly in her spirit. "A bunch of age-old prayers *mean nothing to me,*" Angel professed recently. Marked vows of adultery and idolatry, these so-called church weddings are not a guarantee for a successful marriage. Angel fears this. Oh God!

Nevertheless, this doesn't mean Angel would like to exclude God's involvement—on the contrary. In fact, it's with all her heart she wants God's blessings. What Angel wouldn't?

But fear of the world's rejection or disapproval of being an unwed mother has clouded, confounded, and confused Angel's spiritual clarity. And this is how angels fall. The world receives displaced angels. It's a spiritual conflict. The compounded interest on the principle or principality of sin. It's never a lack of knowledge, rather a lack of understanding. You can't serve two masters, and you can't love in fear.

Because fear causes torment. God's perfect love casts fear out. And he, or she, that has fear has not God's perfect love. Angels aren't excluded. Because God is not a respecter of persons.

But fear not my angel! For God is with you, and if God is with you, who can be against you? Remember, seek ye first the kingdom of God within your spirit, and all else will be added.

Then seek understanding and ask for forgiveness and forgive those who have played a role in your early contaminations.

Judge no one. Hate no one. Envy no one. Be jealous of no one. Lust after nothing. Love your husband as yourself. And your husband should love you, for you and he are one. As in the beginning, a man leaves his mother and father and cleaves to his wife and becomes as one flesh (Genesis 2:24).

Raise, regulate, and train your gift from God, **your child.** Guide the child in the ways of the Lord, for the child is the fruit of the womb and is God's reward.

So, my Angel, fear not! Be free and embrace the spiritual righteousness of a living God. The God of love, for that is God's will and his love. The law of matrimony. For marriage is unto God. The marriage is with God. Therefore, let no man, woman, or child put this union asunder. It is ungodly.

So! *Shake it up, baby!* But don't get **ALL SHOOK UP!**

Amen!

Good Morn'n

I had just crawled back into bed, snuggled smooth as a groove up to my darlin' wife of thirty-eight years to date wonderful, faith-developing years. It was an "*In the Moment*" realization that pure faith had carried us through the years. *Pure faith*—smoothing out our many flaws *and* still we're working it out. *We ain't flawless!* But we are smoother, happier, more in touch with our lives because we are keeping our hearts in close proximity to each other. We continually fulfill *Our Father's* divine will that we keep our full armor of faith on, for the work never stops, not until you hear, "Job well done, my good and faithful servant."

All this is flowing through my head, the memories, the recollections of experiences my mind had tucked away, all come flooding over me. My thoughts erupted in an epiphany of revelation—an *aha!* Hmm . . . so that's what all this is! What it be like keepin' it real. The acceptance of the actualization of the moment. A true perspective of the truth—the trials and errors. The tribulation is what our reality realistically consists of the "*I'll be dammed*" and the *"Ain't this a bitch! This shit IS real!"* Like spasms, the epiphany keeps on erupting! Now the revelations begin to get thorny—like SIN! The fall in the Garden where Adam failed to stay on top of the situation. Failed! He blew it! Me, *myself, and I*—included!

All of this, all **In the Moment**, leads me down into a heart of light. A spiritual insight. An appreciation of a world moving out of control. I am a part of the spiritual world's   worldwide   dysfunctionality—a   *sin*-fullness syndrome. The proof, clinically speaking, is that it's a birth *D-fect.* It's in ev'vabody's DNA. Remember, we all fall! Even the *born-again.* Since the sins of the fathers are recycled through yo' mamas drama. This is a confession! *I AM* is the spirit convicting me. Predisposed, I give it up. I confess. I am da' problem! A confession of truth—the solution.

I guarantee you, once this axiom is accepted, then understood, the principle of the light goes on—*within*! **Click!** Then and only then does your spirit know for sure that you're a reflection of the light. It's a wake-up call. *Hello!* Wake up, ev'vabody! **Wake up!**

The call for me to wake up came at approximately 3:00 AM—give or take an exact time line—that's not the issue. *Time* itself is of the essence. *Time* is precious, and the *time* we have in this life can be fleeting . . . like childhood. In the blink of an eye, **Gone!** So when God wakes you up, it's always on *Now* time! *Time* is irrelevant to God. *Time* is like faith; it's *right NOW!* And *right HERE!* Like *now,* answering the phone at 3:00 AM.

The phone rang several times. I was a little foggy, coming into focus after having stayed up late watching the Beijing 2008 Olympics. The images of the night before flashed back into my mind. A lot of the participants who were favored to win were getting their international E-gos spanked. *S and M'd—serious meltdowns!* The inner pressure of overcompensating one's national patriotic cultivated church and state racial pride leads to the *haughty fall.* Trying to balance on the beam of greatness making *His-Story* is heavy! The side effects can get you *baton-whipped,* ending up with the dropsies. Got Drop-I-tis and hurdle-slapped and, adding insult to injury, line dancing disqualification!

Click! Reality check! This doesn't have any real significant connection with my phone ringing at 3:00 AM; however, rolling over, I look at my wife, Sue. She's such a wonderful gift. A gift wrapped with love inside and out! A gracious gift proving God is good.

"Good morn'n, can I be of service?" I always answer the phone in a spirit of service, automatically. Sincerity has a flare, a ring. *Can I be of service?* This is the way the police and the world governments are supposed to act and sound like, which leaves no excuse for parents. *Ouch!*

Listening to the caller's voice, I immediately recognize that it is Steve, one of my students and *spiritual wards.* Steve is a beautiful and intelligent young man. Loving, very sensitive, and one of the most vibrant, artistic, and truthfully honest young men I have had the pleasure to work with; however, he's a man-child yet, an old soul! All of seventeen, he's an impulsive, compulsive, energetic, evolving soul—a son-ny D-Light, which is not the point!

Does this fool have any idea what time it is? I think as I'm 'bout to go Morris Day. Yet I chuckle to myself, listening to Steve's inner excitement, which comes across in a very laid-back way. So cool and collected, very *in* control. Me? I'm feelin' like it's an *X-Files* opening. Some digitally suppressed drama, as I convey the realities of time, space, and need. *Hey! It's 3:00 AM! What's with man-child? I'm tired and want to sleep. I'm under the sheets with my darlin' Sue, she's my bit of heaven.* **Oops, dere it iz!**

Patiently, I adapt, like a loving parent, a friend, and counselor—psychiatric, no doubt! Lovingly, the spirit of truth emerges as a gift from an all-knowing God. His child. The gates of heaven—HERE! On earth! Salvation, a gift for God's children to save the world by faith. It's the child conversion by grace. Born-again prophesy fulfilled. Steve's cup is brim full and running over AND on *fire*! *Praise da' Lord!* But hey, it's 3:00 *AM!*

Steve and I are very close—relationship-wise. We enjoy a tight bond of love. An *agape love,* the kind that cements a cherished spiritual kinship. The gift of love by grace. Love is something Steve so desperately wants to share and explore with a peer. A friend—a very sweet young lady whom Steve admires and adores—is, in his eyes, the perfect woman and the one whom he may want to marry one day. Definitely to cherish and honor in friendship.

I had the great pleasure and privilege to meet this young lady. I also had the pleasure of meeting her mother and younger brother. I met each of them at Steve's grandfather's funeral. The cemetery was up in a beautiful section of the Hollywood Hills.

Afterward, at the home of Steve's mother and father came an opportunity to celebrate, mourn, and honor the passing of Steve's father's father. It was now that Steve and this beautiful young lady would begin to see each other through a different set of eyes. Conversation was light, yet the depth and intensity of the moment gave me the distinctive honor of having a close encounter—*lights, camera, roll 'em, action!* We were caught up in the *rapture* of the moment.

Their relationship mirrored their private lives—behind closed doors. Shaken and disturbing, yet somehow, I fit into the mix—the conflict. As the plot thickens, she flips the script on Steve. It came when he tried to explain *our* relationship. Now, *X-Files* and *X-Factor* merge to become *the* subplot. She flip-flopped. The subplot, the confession, as Steve related to her how much he had confided in me his joy and his pains.

A **big** mistake! He knows now! I can hear it in the tone of his voice. He's not radiating; he's not so cool or so together. The wall of self-confidence is crumbling, and he literally begins to cry. His tears escalate into sobbing as he spills out his true confession. It has become difficult for me to understand what he's saying to me on the phone because he's become incoherent. Yet through the flow of tears, he says, "Mick E., I told her everything! That I kissed you on the mouth!" There is a momentary hush! I literally take the phone away from my ear, though I still hear him crying.

In tears, he says, "Mick E., I love you!" He sort of blurts it out, as if he hadn't wanted to say it but said it anyway! Then came the **da-dum!** "You're the only person who cares about me. You can hear me. Even when I don't speak, you read my soul. You stopped me from committing suicide," he cries out. Then he asks, "We're not weird, are we? She said our relationship was weird. When I told her a man had taught me how to love." I was startled by his revelations! He was shaken by his own words! There was a deafening silence as we each sorted out our thoughts.

Not being a mind reader, I wasn't able to know what exactly was to come next; however, I intuitively realized that this was **In the Moment** when the Holy Spirit within would offer up the truth exactly as Steve needed to hear it.

I said, tentatively at first, "Yes, we are weird and extremely peculiar to her! And to whoever else sees us like she does, for example, yo' mama 'n her mama 'n whoever else lookin ova' our shoulder." I paused for a moment feeling his presence surround me. I spread my wings and said, "Those judging us from the voyage of their own perverted, sordid darkness—whether the judges are your peers, the young or old, the left or right, the gay—the never truthfully straight, whatever or whomever. It's just their void, an absence of Love. This is why light and dark don't mix. They ain't jell'n, just yell'n 'n raisin' hell'n because judges confuse sex with love. Love is love, not sex; in fact, it's circumstantial evidence versus the truth."

Feeling the freedom of spiritual flight, I knew I was headed into his heart as I said, "I realize you have deep and true congenial feelings for this sweet young lady. You love her, which is so beautiful. That's a good thing! Owe no one nothing . . . except love. However, and for the most part, the exclusive bottom line is that she doesn't have the capacity or the knack nor a clue how to graciously receive the virtue of your sincerity. She's a fallen soul still! And isn't awake or ready to ascend up to be the blessed recipient of the righteousness of truth, a confession. Pure and true. No hidden agendas."

I took another breath and knew the Holy Spirit was within me. I knew he'd hear the word, for the word was coming from him and not me. For Steve, these are the true words. For others, it is an enlightenment or a light in the dark for those who haven't grasped the truth of *agape love*. The Holy Spirit used me to convey these truths for Steve to perceive, as well as for those he loves. Then out it came.

"You're baring your soul to her. In truth and spirit. For you, it's a catharsis, a relief, a cleansing! For her, it's overbearing, too much light for her darkened and damaged interior soul to conceive, let alone receive! She's weak in faith and riddled with anger, frustration, and depression. Green with envy and resentment. She's in despair.

"*The Two Faces of Eve*. She might be Sibyl—severely and spiritually damaged. Psychologically traumatized 'n living in the house of pain with Mommy dearest. Now like the world, *it's a ball of confusion*. Therefore, I conclude that love is a stretch and for the unloved, a strain. Which makes sense? Why? For her and many others, our relationship is weird—a loving spiritual relationship between a sixty-six-year-old man and a seventeen-year-old man-child."

I held the receiver away from my head 'cause I could feel it comin' as I spoke into the mouthpiece, "Get real, son! This has the sound of an altar boy and the priest doing the ben-a-dick-shun. Hail Mary! Full of grace 'n here comes Jesus. I feel her, I know you've felt her! This is not the first time you've been to confession. Praise the Lord!"

On a more conciliatory note, I said, "Oddly enough, Steve, the core of this relationship is ageless and timeless. It's a uniting spirit . . . our love . . . one love . . . not a generation gap. It's un-gapped. It's in the same spiritual time zone of the one all-knowing universal God of agape love."

> *And though I have the gift of prophecy and understand all mysteries and all knowledge and though I have faith so that I could remove mountains, but have not love, I am nothing. And though I bestow all my goods to feed the poor, and though I give my body to be burned, but haven't love, it profits me nothing. Love suffers long and is kind. Love does not envy. Love does not parade itself, is not puffed up and does not behave rudely, does not seek its own, is not provoked, thinks no evil, does not rejoice in iniquity, but rejoices in the truth; bears all things, believes all things, hopes all things, endures all things. Love never fails. But whether there are prophecies, they*

will fail; whether there are tongues, they will cease;
whether there is knowledge, it will vanish away. For
we know in part and we prophesy in part. But when
that which is perfect has come, then that which is in
part will be done away. When I was a child, I spoke
as a child, I understood as a child, I thought as a
child; but when I became a man, I put away childish
things. For now we see in a mirror, dimly, but then
face to face. Now I know in part, but then I shall
know just as I also am known. And now abide faith,
hope and love, these three; but the greatest of these is
love.

1 Corinthians 2-13

For God so loved the world that he gave his only
begotten Son, . . .

John 3:16

The Word. Manifested for us to abide in. Which is love.
Jesus, the Lord and law. In the spirit of *agape love,* he said,

If you abide in my word you are my disciples indeed.
And you shall know the truth. And the truth will set
you free.

John 8:31

So freely I speak, my brother and family, to you in the
spirit and of truth. Unequivocally, I say,

I will continue to kiss you over and over. It's my holy kissing duty. It is written: "Greet all the brethren with a holy kiss."

1 Thessalonians 5:26

How you like this Scripture?

Greet one another with a holy kiss. The churches of Christ greet you.

Romans 16:16

Ahh! That's so refreshing when one is true to the authentic self. Converted, as a man-child of the Most High God of agape, universal Love. The spirit of truth.

And it's all joy, this good-morning call. By faith. For I heard the voice of God in the sound of your voice, Steve. Thanks for the good morn'n, a wake-up call of love. I call it a joy. Praise God, for ***It is written . . .***

Sing praises to the Lord, you saints of his. And give thanks at the remembrance of his holy name. For his anger is but for a moment. his favor is for life; weeping may endure for a night, but joy comes in the morning.

Psalm 30:5

Let him who is taught the word share in all good things with him who teaches.

Galatians 6:6

As it was in the beginning, it is now Good morn'n! Can I be of service . . . *with much love.*

A CORRESPONDENCE
LAPSE

Greetings, my brother!

I've always loved saying that. Literally, I was raised to believe and call all men and boys, *brother.* My mother always stressed that there were no cousins or in-laws in Christ. She claimed this was the purpose Jesus had in teaching us to pray, *Our Father.* Not *my daddy.* My mother said this was God's way of bringing the family together. She said it's the *Family Prayer,* not the Lord's Prayer. "If the Lord need a prayer, who is he praying to?" she would say.

While lapsing back into *motherhood memories,* I am looking at a letter from my wife's brother, J. Michael Sullivan. He is writing about Sue's current battle with another phase of her epilepsy. He'd witnessed a few of Sue's many convulsions. I too have been up close and personal with numerous convulsions. In fact, on our first serious date, Sue had one.

She thought that this would surely end our relationship. Because in previous relationships, this was always the deal breaker. *See ya', wouldn't wanna' be ya'!* But not me! Sue was made to order! A prayer-line special, for I had in private gone into my closet to talk with the Lord. I wanted to discuss marriage. God's sacred institution of his union with the human race. A marriage of Creator with his creation through the resurrection of Christ Jesus—the Bridegroom. This is how we're *born again.* It's a spiritual impregnation—an immaculate conception. It happens when you invite Jesus to come into your life and impregnate you with his Holy Spirit. You become wedded to him in the spirit, and your life becomes a mirror of the love and devotion going on inside of you. It's a concept unique in all the world. It is truly ecstatic and divine. A serious natural high. You'll be on cloud nine, rolling around heaven all day and all night. It's a real upper having accepted Christ into your life, for he will be there when we fall, and we all do.

I'm *In the Moment!* I feel it—this timelessness of NOW. I remember distinctly asking *Our Father* in private, "Father, I'm ready for marriage. A marriage that honors you. I want to get in bed with you and let's get it on! Father, you know the woman I want to have intercourse with you. I want Christ to fill my heart, my loins, my being with his very essence transferring this to my woman, my wife, my partner in life. So send me the woman I need who will help bring me closer to you."

And God, the all-knowing *Our Father,* sent me an epileptic white woman! What a sense of humor. *Praise God.*

Yoke on! See, you know that God *is not a respecter of persons! So . . . walk by faith! Not by sight! Black or white!*

God's love is unbounded, and his humor is up close and personal. I share his love in me in my greeting of universal brotherhood. I share with my sisters and brothers in the universe. *The All!* Jesus was born, died, and resurrected for us. Because *Our Father,* God, the one and almighty, forgiving, loving, merciful God is the only one who knows my heart. As a confessed sinner, I confessed the resurrection of that redeeming, restoring love of God, *Our Father's* family—the *human race*—in that I am humbled and privileged to be a part of God's restoration of the family plan. As it was in the beginning—***family.*** Mankind and his kind are one and the same—***NOW!*** This *is pro life . . . pro love.*

This is why I love saying, "Greetings, my brother!" It's a family thing to do. Loving you! I love saying that. That's why I write you, J. Michael Sullivan, in the spirit of brotherhood. It is my sentiment as I correspond with you, Sue's biological brother, and my brother through his grace. I have always been about love . . . with you. That's what I do, I'm *lover man.* As you can see, I'm *still in* love with you. You're more Sue's twin than Fran. By the way, love covers all sin, did you know that? Love . . . not lust. There *is* a difference. The covenant of *Our Father's* love binds the family. Lust loosens.

The difference is most people can't distinguish between the two. Creating gender confusion. Same sex abuse. Some say it's inborn. Maybe? I believe it's a conscious choice within our inner dialog—our thinking. This is why Scripture says, *"Watch your thinking."* This is why I'm always thinking of love. See, I have thought it out. Love a confession of itself! Pure and simple—the truth.

This is a true confession, by the way. You know, don't you, that I am a confessed sinner. However, sin is *not* my master. This is where love comes in. This is my spiritual exoneration. By grace comes freedom and the truth. *Our Father's* will being done. The forgiveness to the spiritual law. Love. The Proverb.

> *Hatred stirs up strife,*
> *But love covers all sins.*
>
> Proverbs 10:12

I know . . . you were probably expecting, or at least hoping for, a response from your twin *(smile)*, and believe me, she would love to have written you back. Unfortunately, Sue is being challenged on a day-to-day basis. To put it bluntly, her bout with epilepsy is psychologically taking its toll. It's been a long-waged war that erupted by its invasion during those formidable transition years of preadolescence and adulthood. Those impressionable stages of life that often define us or redefine us. Usually, a combination of the two. Something is usually lost in the transition.

It's during these stages of transformation when traumatic events make indelible imprints on the psychic self. The core of a person's inner being. The heart and soul of who we think we are, our concept of *self.* Shattered in the trauma and the drama. Torn asunder, virtually destroying her *authentic self.* That's who I live with, and my brother, that's who I love! Your sister! A human being, an epileptic white woman—*a gift!*

I have really come to admire, respect, love, and deeply treasure *our* Sue. A precious commodity. The broken and downtrodden Sue has taken some big hits in life. No different than being hit and run over, then abandoned and left by the side of the road . . . to die. I sometimes feel like a passenger in a car witnessing, then drives on by.

The irony of seeing this has strengthened my faith. My human compassion has grown deeper as a caretaker. The spiritual understanding more profound. It's very humbling. The spirit of love. God's will being done. A true confession of love. It's the saving grace, the ingredient very few, self included, use to its full capacity.

Sue is very depressed, scared, and carries deep wounds from the formidable years of rejection and being psychologically ostracized. *She married me!* Damaged more than any sibling or so-called friend will ever truly know or perhaps cares to know.

Remember, Sue broke down during the 1983 childbirth, right under family members' and so-called friends' eyes? Postpartum depression. Remember? Ring a bell? After all, it was you who made the *9/11 ground zero* call. You called Hollywood for an unlikely hero, *the Black Knight*—**me!** When the movie comes out, it will be titled *The Miracle at 1209 Boylston Street.*

That was then, and this is now. Sue's now dealing with another characteristic of epilepsy. *Myoclonic* jerks. A lot of little convulsive jerks. A lot like world governments. Uncontrollable. This is why she fell, like the economy, and broke her toe. Damaged her shoulder and back. It's frustrating and debilitating. Sue sometimes has the look of a dazed fighter who just got his *bell rung*. The medication has rough side effects. Balance, drowsiness, loss of memory, and at times, illegible handwriting. Medication the side effect symptom! The ill-lusion. The real culprit. The predator, the alien. Is Alzheimers! The silent assassin. What's up, Doc?

So your letter was a welcomed comfort to her. *Thank you.* It was a needed *C-R-C 4-U,* i.e., *correspondence response communication 4-understanding.* The matters of the heart. C-R-C 4-U symbolizes the signs and wonders with which to behold the mysteries, questions, and answers revealed for freedom from this pain. When the truth by love unfolds, it is a healing manifestation. A true confession of love. *It is written . . .*

A true confession of love. To go beyond. To get outside the box, which is ourself. Our E-go. Pride stripped is always the beginning of peace. It starts within. When we realize we're a part of the *problem,* we instantly become the *solution.* This is the key to why violence is so often domestic. It's home grown, becoming justified, commercialized, and mainstream, as only humans can rationalize. *Ultimate fighting* has become a cultural tradition and politically correct. Now the church and sad state—a world crises. It's all in the mix. Beginning in childhood. The part of the *humane* experience that's deeply misunderstood. Why? We are the world. Following the world playbook. The silver lining playbook. Yeah! Hollywood is playing "us," making us characters in their playbook. They casting and playing us as Twilighter's DC. Politically correct—zombies! Now! We Hansel and Gretel! Salem. Witch hunters. The dysfunctional! Give me mah gun or off wit'cha head. The criminally un-sane! Our world leaders and the everyday people. Son-a-Bitches the normal-shameless bitches! This movie will be rated RS—real sick. Make sure your kids see this. It's family friendly. Hooray! For Hollywood! Gotcha!

People say children are the future. Well! The future looks a little hung up. This is why God, *Our Father*, puts so much emphasis on childhood. For example, Jesus took a little child and set him in the midst of them, and when he had him in his arms, he said,

> *Whoever receives one of these little children in my name receives me; and whoever receives me, receives not me but him who sent me.*
>
> Mark 9:37

What about this one . . .

> *Let the little children come to me, and do not forbid them; for of such is the kingdom of God.*
>
> Mark 10:14

And finally,

Train up a child in the way he should go. And when he is old, he will not depart from it.

Proverbs 22:6

And being that we are all children of the Most High *Our Father*, it has come full circle. With love, caring, and sharing through the gift of *love*. Christ by whose stripes we were healed. I believe I can conclude with this scripture reference, "You will surely say this proverb to me, physician, heal thyself!"

THANKS 4 THE MEMORIES

H ello! And a gracious salutation of love toward you and yours. So how is your health and spiritual security doing, *sweetheart?* How has the *soul journey* of life been thus far?

Hold it!

Before we journey further, let me *clarify* a few things right now. These notes are spontaneous heart streams, which are active streams of conscious love, amorously inspired by deep reflections. However, you gotta understand one thing. I'm a self-confessed *grammatically challenged* retard. This self-confession in no way dilutes my message nor diminish the love that rises from my heart, rather or perhaps in spite of this affliction, never am I at a loss for self-expression.

The execution that lay before you conveys, demonstrates, and constitutes the whole of my being. The *who* of who I am. The one who is emancipated. Free! A free being who is accountable for the privilege and *freedom* of being one whose very motif is responsive to the will of God and his divine expression: **LOVE**. Therefore, I never experience *writer's block*, which doesn't excuse my *grammatical retardation*. This is why I have an editor. *(Yeah, God is great! His spirit spontaneous. His love eternal!* **Editor**.*)*

As I was saying, I find that grammar can be like the infrastructure of the government—complex and confusing. On the other hand, it's a lot like science and math, which to me is like a foreign language. Taking this and interpreting the political application through interpersonal relationships, then figuratively speaking, avoiding the subtlety of the *Willie Goes Round in Circles* syndrome, can somehow degenerate into a bad form of *deja vu. Whew!* The social implications are obvious to me. The political significance apparent. It's the recycling aspect—the return to the future—the circle of life, where details change but the principality remains the same. History repeating itself—the stage of life—theater in the round. This bitter earth.

How you like me now? I'm back to writing you. Interesting stuff, huh? Interest is an invested concern for another. A consideration of one's invested self toward another. A deposit in the spiritual bank of principle and integrity. I believe it's called *Love*. A *love* governed by faith. Based on a belief system founded on the intuitive, sincere desire to care. Caring for another regardless of the return or circumstances. *Love* never undermines true intent! *Yum! Yum!*

Love is the doing unto others as you would have done unto you—a patriotic act of honesty. A spiritual *Code of Conduct* monitored by TRUTH. A wholeness. A privileged freedom. So God can help **us** understand to self-examine and be responsible, then accountable for our behavior. The choices and the consequences as well as the repercussions. Negative, positive, indifferent, good, bad, and, even evil. I confess, I don't know about you, but this is vital to my soul. This is *soul food!*

Aha! It's a confession. Confessing one to another. It's forgiveness. It's trust. For this is how the truth functions. Especially during a crisis when the mentally stressful and psychologically spiritual dysfunctional dramas and traumatic events arise in and on the journey. We've both been there and have survived with reasonable self-dignity. *We still here—intact!* Made out to be a villain from time to time, yet not castrated and able to **forgive**. Always to *love!*

With pen in hand, I allow *love* to flow; for as it was in the beginning, there's no end to *Love*. It's the law of the spirit. A universal declaration to the *hu-man race!* One family, one people, one purpose—to *Love*. It's in the DNA of the spirit. It's divine integration—a diversity of O N E. A united hu-man response, a divine revelation. The epiphany of harmonious living. Love thy neighbor, and who is thy neighbor?

> One living or located near another. Being immediately adjoining or relatively near. (*Merriam Webster Deluxe Dictionary*)

According to that, yo' wife, kids, next-door neighbor, and any other means or situation that puts you or another in immediate or adjoining spaces that are relatively near is a neighbor! That covers a whole lot of ground, *if* truly taken literally! This is why you know Christians are the hypocritical kings of the religious lot because the second most powerful commandment is **"Love thy neighbor,"** which covers everybody. That is why Jesus said, "I came for all . . ." Howdy, neighbor! *Love yo' neighbor,* or there will be no peace. No justice. Just war and chaos. It's a side effect of daily living. This is why the **Good News** is never good. It's not the light of spiritual understanding of the law of love, but rather a tell-a-vision event. A sight we *see* rather than faith we *believe.*

This is why you walk by faith and not by the sight of tell-a-vision and the visual effects it produces. This is why faith comes by *hearing.* Not the cacophony of human noise generated by sight, but by **hearing the Word of God. It is written . . .** Can you hear me now? I love you, J. Michael. Always did. Always will. It's the law!

Love the brotherhood . . .

1 Peter 2:17

Can you feel the love, bro-tha-man? That's what you are: *a good man!* It's an honor to know you and to be a brother of yours!

By the way, it's two in the morning, and I'm sitting here by candlelight confessing *love.* This ain't a sermon nor preaching—it's reaching. Reaching out to my *brother* while reminiscing about special times, which are to me *sacred times.* As I journey back to an earlier **us**, I'm listening to Eddie Kendricks (one of the original Temptations) singing, "Baby girl you need a change of mind baby girl you need a change of mind."

I'm thinking, change is inevitable—like a marriage—it changes for better or worse, good or evil, right or wrong. "One day young . . . the next day, old. A change is gonna come . . . ," sang by Sam Cooke.

Relationships change like people, yet something remains the same, and that's the internal *conflict* of how to *love.* Oddly enough or perhaps by fate, when it comes to *love,* I never change.

Why? *Love* is the foundation and only the details change. The circumstances change, but the principle remains the same. When it is spiritual *love,* it can sustain, endure, and won't diminish or pale by comparison. It will stand like a *beacon of light.* Brilliant, bright, and be a refuge. A soft place to fall in the turbulent times of life. *Love*—a faith greater than circumstance. Rising above the *bullshit* and the *baggage* we all carry or sometimes lug around. Most deny it—*the dark side.* This is why I keep the *light of love* always on. I'm like the Motel Six—click!

That brings me back to what I've been attempting to express sitting here in the dark, by candlelight, reflecting on you . . . or *us.* We were once an item of concern. Our relationship, which includes Sue, who had to endure and put into perspective the nature of our mutual relationships. It is part of the journey of divine understanding. The truisms of truths—reality. Never an extreme, simply what it is, **is** what it is! ***Oops, dere it iz!***

How do you handle it? *Duh* (smile), you don't! You let go and let God! I'm not trying to be heavy, evangelical, intellectual, witty, or catty. I'm trying to be frank, free, and forthright—to the point.

Now, speaking of your daddy, Frank. I had a few precious, if not subtle, moments with him—your father—and it was all good. When I think about yo' daddy, naturally, I have to think about yo' mama. My gal Peggy. *Queen Peggy.* Her Majesty—a figure of grandeur in her *royal-ness.* She was pomp and splendor; plus she was funny. We had a few belly laughs—seriously! *(Ha, ha . . .)*

I enjoyed both yo' mama and yo' daddy thoroughly. Love is like that. It doesn't judge. It confronts and faces the flaws; gets the best and leaves the rest in its own spiritual mess. Shit happens, and we reap what we sow. So! Watch your thinking . . . for as we think, so it is! Free will. *Pro* choice. Free Willie.

I remember when I chose yo' presence to love. It was my spiritual choice and a very conscious decision. It wasn't a premeditated, but rather a natural response—spontaneous. Sincere, open, and entirely honest—***In the Moment!*** The discovery of reality as *the truth* exposes motivation and hidden agendas. *Love,* a serious and vital indicator of how the truth is gonna go . . . *the revelation.*

The first time we encountered each other was in New York—9/11. Only this was pre-9/11—the 411—*yeah!* This would be a very informative first night. A stiff introduction.

A cold New York minute. No Kong. No King. However, there was *the queen*—yo' mama. And you were her official driver, the chauffeur, an earlier version of Driving Miss Daisy, upscaled.

This is New York: **Manhattan!** Technically, we were on the borderline of Harlem. Well, to some, Harlem. It depends on who's callin' "The Tech." New York, New York—the *Statute of Limitations. Our* first encounter was symbolically indelible. It's forever stamped in my mind and always on my heart. My *love for you,* my brotha'! A fond memory. Thanks!

We gathered at your sister Fran's and her husband Richard. They are the Houses, and this was their wonderful *House & Garden* apartment. The apartment was artistic and refreshing. It looked like some of Oprah's makeover people had been there. Okay, I won't go there, but it was charming.

So much for the arts—it was a gathering. A minitrial, if you will. A tribunal, if you can recall the aura of this historical, hysterical evening. Guess Who's Coming to Dinner to be judged, scrutinized, and evaluated? The panel was Fran, Rich, and yo' mama. She was the figurehead, proving royalty had its place by providing us a monarchy in a democratic society. Don King . . . *only in America!* You gotta love it, like I love you. *Oh, say can you see . . .*

I know, through the purple haze of this tribunal, I could see you. You were a part of the audience, a member of the Sideline Players Co. Sort of like a couch potato under protection of the witness protection program. In a league of your own.

You, Sue, and my cousin, Pat Allen, who at times was working on his doctorate at Harvard University. This was a classic. My trial—a tribulation of love ala *New York, New York.* A renaissance memorial moment. A keepsake.

Time would pass, literally marching on. In the march, you and I seemed to find a rhythmic stride, which drew us closer. We seemed to be tuned into and in step with our inner selves. Our relationship had a feel and a look of closeness; it seemed very open. It looked that way, but as you know, looks are deceiving, and things are never as they appear.

In time, events would turn to reveal the real deal about us at the core, in the heart. This was life-defining stuff . . . the experience. Really, it was all good—for us. Always dignified as events recycled our relationship. The phenomena of *love* is always a comfort. It never fails in a crisis. This is why! Jesus is a crisis fighter. It's the Christ-A most. This is why "freedom" rings.

Like the time you called from that resort. I believe it was Hyannis Port. You called *crying* like a baby—distraught, shattered, and devastated. It was a crying shame! I got past the crybaby stuff, but what you couldn't get past was the reality of being fired. Dismissed and kicked to the curb or beachfront as it were. Fired, discharged! *Why?* You had let your mouth write a check your ass couldn't cash. So you were terminated. Yo' ass gotta go!

Now the plot thickens like a Charles Dickens's *Ebenezer Screws* scenario. You are *Bob Cratchit* and *Tiny Tim*. You were like a crippled crab without a crutch. So who do you call? Me! Because you couldn't call home. Greenwich—the White House. Naw! You called 1209 Boylston Street, Boston. *Crispus Attucks . . .* me!

The real problem wasn't you being fired; it was facing your father. Frankly speaking, this was your greatest fear. This is what *the cryin'* was all about. The crying shame of facing yo' daddy. In desperation, you called Sam Spade—***the Boston Tar Baby***. 'Cause black really **is** beautiful . . . white on!

When I heard that stressed-out, pitiful cry, my initial response was, "Come home!" Bid your associate friends *farewell, adiós, and good-Bye.* See ya'all later, alligator, and after a while crocodile. Then I encouraged you to embrace the experience as *a wake-up call* to immaturity, ego, and false pride. Class dismissed!

Through experience, life teaches one about being full of *piss and vinegar.* The sour grapes of Martha's Vineyard. Smellin' yo' own shit. **The Lesson:** How to smell the funk then comprehend its fun-kay-ness—the oxymoron paradoxical principle. Get it? You reap what you sow. The laws of cause and effect. Murphy's law. Shit happens! And ignorance of the law doesn't excuse anyone. The law doesn't discriminate. That's why it rains on the just and the unjust alike. The innocent, the guilty, and the naive. Point in case, we all fall short, regardless of how clever, bright, brilliant, rich, dumb, or poor we think we are.

Whether blind, crippled, and crazy, and we can be all of
that; nevertheless, there's an old scriptural saying, "Pride
goes before destruction [self], a haughty spirit before a fall."
Plop! Plop! Fizz . . . fizz . . .

And the night was clear. The moon was yellow. The
leaves came tumbling down. Which is neither here nor
there, so to continue my refrain . . . There you were, on
the phone, sobbing. Literally embarrassed and humiliated,
without a clue as to why you got fired. Stupidity and
arrogance is like that. They're characteristics of youth.

According to you, as I listened to your side of the story,
leading up to that *moment of martyrdom* when you learned
your service was no longer needed, and you had less than
twenty-four hours for your physical presence to be like,
gone!

Then you tell me about *plan B,* your *ace in the hole!* You
tell me it's founded on the First Amendment! After all, this
is America! A democratic society with free speech, the Bill
of Rights, and it was the '70s, plus being white. Hail to da'
chief . . . cry freedom. I'm doin' my thing and to hell with
the establishment! **Shout!** Say it loud! It's all good . . . the
result: **FIRED!** See ya'! Wouldn't want to be ya'! 'Cause yo'
ass is scared to death. *(Mostly fired, I fear.)*

Sympathetically, I listened to you, taking it all into
account. I said, "Stop cryin'. *Come home, sweetheart!"*
Then there was silence. It felt like a scene from *Bambi.*
The silence dramatically broken by sobbing as you
spasmodically, almost convulsively, attempted to catch your

breath, sobbing, "Why did they fire me?" I responded by saying, "Michael! Come home!" and hung up.

I sat still with my eyes closed, rockin' back and forth, like Ray Charles. I smiled as I meditated on the following:

> *You who fear the Lord, trust in the Lord. He is their help and their shield.*
>
> Psalm 115:11

Then, I brought it all home with:

> *I can do all things through Christ who strengthens me.*
>
> Philippians 4:13

Bingo!

A solution had been found. It was actually a simple solution. The problem was solved by my **faith**. I acted on the **Word**. *So* I say to myself: *Self . . .*

> *Ask and it will be given to you; seek and you will find; knock and it will be opened to you for everyone who asks receives, and he who seeks finds, and to him who knocks it will be opened.*
>
> Luke 10:9-10

Shazzam! I reach for the telephone. I dialed with great expediency and a glad heart, for this was joy—the residual of the solution. An immediate resolution. Just in the nick of time. No problem. *Praise the Lord.*

The phone rings. I'm a bit excited. Oh! I was giving up the glory. Oh, happy days! What a friend we have in the compassion of Christ, always throwing out a blessing when you truly . . .

Love the brotherhood.

1 Peter 2:17

"Hello." It's the sound of Dr. Offey Edom, the African veterinarian, the black Dr. Doolittle who is about to do more than he might ever expect.

"What's happen'n, Dr. D. What's up, Doc?" He began to laugh like he knew som'em up!

He chimes in, asking, "What can I do for you, my brotha?" and just burst out laughing with a great joy.

It's a *brotha'* thing—a contagious sort of laughter born of truth among believers. The honesty and knowing when spirits are true to themselves—no problem. You become *a solution resolution. Free at last! Thank God Almighty!*

Then Dr. D., freely and without reservation or hesitation, cleared his throat and probed, "My brotha', what do you need?" An **aha** escaped my lips as I realized this was the perfect lead in . . . need. The key! So I open right up, asking, "Do you need any help there?" I emphasized *any,* praying with fingers, toes and eyes crossed, that the doctor would say, "I need someone badly . . . soon! Like, right now!" Dr. D. yelled, "My gawd, do I!" Hearing that was an adrenaline rush! "Well, brotha', I have what you need! A strong big young body, and it's white!" "Um-gawah!" I howled.

The doctor laughed hysterically. But before he would confirm, he morphed and became somewhat diplomatic and very professional, with a very somber disposition. A discernment check with a spiritual nature. A background soul check. I may have been his brotha', but that was not the issue. This is business. His business, and he's not about to jeopardize it by throwing his pearls befo' the feet of swine. So we engaged in a piggy-wiggly background checkout. Bugs Bunny can come, but Porky Pig need not apply. *Oink . . . oink!* Now, this is real pig Latin . . . *no oinking!*

The swine inquiry had two parts:

1. What kind of person is he?
2. Is he like Sue?

I could easily see the inquiry was simply stated, but it was the undertone, the subtle subtext that would prove very deep. What a criteria for hiring. A job qualification based on the *man-woman Genesis* revelation. A comparison analogy of the same in spirit. God's family traits. His DNA.

Speaking deliberately and in a very matter-of-fact tone, I said, There's no one to me like Sue. On the other hand, this young man possesses a lot of the qualities and spiritual substance of Sue. He's reliable, for the most part. A good worker. Trustworthy, sensitive in the caring sense. Loves animals, except snakes, but . . ." There was a pause of the pregnant kind as the doctor delivered his coups da grace qualifier. "Would you hire him?" he mused.

This was a no-brainer, I thought, as I replied, "Yes, I love him. He's my brotha'!" Evidently, this was the piece de resistance. It was a done deal. Except for finalizing hours and wages. The most pertinent clarification. If memory serves me correctly, I negotiated a substantial raise—with unbelievable working and living conditions. Most importantly, solitude—regrouping and healing time.

So, Michael! By the time you arrived at 1209 Boylston Street—*home*—and unbeknownst to you, you had a new job with *Perks*. You never know who your angels are—*Joy to the World*—except, there was no joy in Mudsville. You wuz in da' blues, deluded into believing the Mighty Casey had not only struck out but was fired! The unemployment blues! Shattered egotism is like that—very blue!

It was so apparent. I felt the funk of your blues as soon as you rang the doorbell. Even the elevator seemed affected by it. Its doors seemed to moan as you exited. The doors clanged and banged shut with a gloomy melancholy affirmation. This was *da' blues*. I started to hear a few B. B. King riffs going through my head.

Despair and defeat. An ego-deflated blues beat. Your death row walk revealed all. The blues step'n by the sound of your feet. *Dead man walk'n'*. The blues—sour and sweet. Sooner or later, the beat repeats, like America's history—*da' red, white, 'n blues!*

Finally, there you were. Standing in front of me. Eyes searching—searching one another—words unspoken, yet we were speaking and addressing the pain. Silence is golden, especially on a blue note.

The blues is a teaching tool of life by its repetitious refrain. So bang the drums slowly. The blues—always for whom the bell tolls. This is classic brotherhood. This is a Hallmark and Kodak moment in *freeze frame*.

Standing there in the doorway, we embraced. You were like a whipped puppy. Head hung with tail between your legs. You buried your head in my chest. Like a baby suckling his mother's breast. Brotherhood at its best! We cried—*boyz do cry!*—and I kissed your tears as you blubbered out, "Why did they fire me?"

I closed the door behind us as we walked down the hallway, passed the bedroom, and the upright piano, into the living room. You placed your bags by the round table—the same round table where we'd dined, wined, broken bread by candlelight, gathered with family: Sue, Nia, Big Deb. Here 'n da' round where we'd had numerous in-depth soul searchings and comparative philosophical exchanges.

It was while standing next to the round table, I answered your question as to why you were fired. Simply stated and to the point, "Your mouth wrote a check yo' ass couldn't cash!" Repetition is learning. It's politically correct, social retardation, it's cultivated. This is why history repeats. It's the DNA of the anti Christ. Its motto "fuck-u" have a nice day.

Brevity is beautiful. No distractions. No confusion, and as you began the process of understanding, it sinks in. I proceeded to the kitchen; opened a bottle of champagne. It was a very fine vintage. If I'm not mistaken, it was Chateau Inexpensive, 1972. If my memory hasn't defected, which is often a side effect of being home alone. **Cheers!**

As I was saying, we smoked a joint, toasted ourselves while we grooved on some Earth, Wind & Fire. I excused myself and went to the bathroom and began drawing you a bath, complete with bubbles and candles. Returning to the living room, I replenished your glass—the green-stemmed crystal glass, I believe. The one your mother, *the queen,* had given us. As you can surely agree, your firing transformed into quite the *royal moment.* Elegant and spiritually delicious! True love is like that!

Watching you like a concerned parent, a proud father, a guardian angel, a delightful brotha', you appeared calmer. Still, there was the cloud of doom hanging over you. You looked worried and haunted by your recent and unexpected job loss. You had lost face. Frankly, cutting to the chase, it was the fear of facing your *daddy*—Frank Sullivan—*the Bomb!* This mushroomed over you like an atomic cloud. A *father-son* fallout! **Boom!**

The radiation of sadness and fear was quickly removed when I announced that you had a job waiting for you. That you were to report for orientation duty tomorrow afternoon. *We have ova' come!* Lift every voice and sing. *We have African connection—roots!* The international hookup. Political asylum from the cloud of fear, doom, and gloom because *Daddy dearest's only male child* got fired from his job! Because you failed to meet the standards of *Daddi-o Sullivan!* Blasphemy! This is not *The Luck of the Irish*—this is the black magic. A celebration! The big payback. It hit me! Good gawd! *Heey!*

All these blessings thanks to our sister Nia's diplomatic foreign policy of universal DNA kinship, Divine Natural Alliance. We toasted Nia and womanhood and savored the spiritual substance, being as we were **In the Moment!** We sang "We Have Overcome" and "Victory Is Ours." God is good! Good God, I'm in the Book of James . . . *Brown!* Good gawd. *Hit me!*

Bubble bathed, cleansed, restored, regenerated, and highly rejuvenated, you began proving how when you walk by faith, when one door closes how another one opens, life changes and can improve. 'Cause God *Our Father* is real! The compassion of Christ. Save the white man. He's my brother. I'm his keeper! *Oh, happy days!* It's in the DNA of God's love. "Love the brotherhood," as referenced in 1 Peter 2:17.

Rejoining us, *Lady Sue,* my precious wife—my queen—helped us feast at the royal roundtable. Now set by grace, we enjoyed a delicious, scrumptious, and fulfilling meal of love. Eating life and drinking *love.* A Lord's Supper! Symbolic of he who died for all. All who believe are invited to partake daily in these precious moments. Gems of clarity. So the truth can set you free. **It is written . . .** Write on!

After a great and peaceful good night of sleep, spiritually reconnected, and well rested, we rose to a refreshed perspective of life. Living in the *Now*. **In the Moment** and keeping it real. Never the extreme.

With all this clarity in the air, it was off to work. It was exciting. I mean, as I reflect on it, I can still feel the excitement of that experience. I'm there right now. Sort of makes me want to whistle, "Hi Ho Hi Ho! It's off to work [we] you go." Yeah! You were Snow White, and I was the eighth dwarf—the blackman. That's deep! *Hi Ho!* I believe this is where the whistling comes in. I'm starting to feel like Jimmy Da' Cricket. This is deeper than I thought. This got some Pinocchio shit it in it. Up yo' nose with a rubber hose. Seriously, though, I ain't lying befo' the hookup. The DNA—**roots!** We talk'n black power, serious spiritual love. Yo' freedom, my humble servitude.

Okay, let's get real. You was living in indigent servitude, a minimum wage, dormitory lifestyle. You wuz a slave! A *step-and-fetch-it* boy! You was rank 'n file . . . in a democratic dictatorship. A *de-mock-racy*. A social mess, especially when you tried, or decided, that your defense would stand on the First Amendment's freedom of expression. Which, need history repeat itself, led to your being fired. You must confess that, but by the grace of God, you were blessed. The luck of the Irish brought you a *black leprechaun*. You got me—the lucky charm! *Mah brotha'. Hey, dude!*

You have to admit you were in a charming situation. Living in Coventry, Rhode Island, with a job, raise, and your own home! And all you had to do was to show up and receive. You was moving on up . . . *home free!* No rent. A house fully loaded and connected to the hospital. You could literally walk to work. You were living large, dude! Plus, you had a bike, so you could run over to Sister Nia's if you got lonely or hungry. You had it all. This is a success story. *Our* brotherhood . . . serious memories for which I am so very thankful. Thank you, my brother, Mr. Sullivan!

It's funny, no matter how everything seems in place and all together, so neatly packaged and tied, there are always some loose ends. Life has a way of coming undone. Unraveling. By some psychological need that needs to be attended to. A psychic red flag. Growth and development—the *art of flag waving.*

The flag would be waved via a phone call one night as you started feeling the pressure of your success. It's lonely at the top. This became evident in spite of your newly acquired good fortune and grandeur. Something unexpected. An element for which you weren't prepared.

The state of being completely alone. No next-door neighbors. *Home alone!* with only yourself. *Solitude* that which gives credence to the fear of being . . . alone with only you! To be home alone with one's consciousness is not always the best company.

Case in point. A lot of people can't stand seclusion with themselves, especially if they're insecure and full of fears. They may find themselves calling out in the middle of the night. Making the stress call, waving the flag and feeling *oh, so alone.*

It was that kind of call I got one night. The flag had been raised, and I could hear the sound of it flapping in the background. This was a **RED ALERT** call! A state of our union. A reality check. A call for a patriotic act of kindness. Always compassion.

Half awake, half asleep. Half baked and halfheartedly hearing the stress call, which came in around twelve—12:30 AM—all I knew was that you were lonely and wanted me to come down. *Like now!* It's like I didn't have a life or a marriage; yet I got up and came. I guess I didn't have a life. On the other hand, the marriage was very intact, intimately tight. We talk'n pre-Viagra, pro Cheerios, Wheaties with the snap, crackle, and pop goes da' weasel!

As I got out of bed, your sister said, "What's up with J. Michael?" I glanced back and saw her calm face, sweet and concerned, and I answered, "He's lonely. Somewhat depressed. He's still in mourning of being fired. Terminated. A death blow to the ego. Basically, it's the longing for the beachfront resort and his cronies. His partners in crime. The ones who encouraged him to express his First Amendment rights. He was their mouthpiece. The sacrificial lamb. They're there, and he's fired. Now he needs his lucky charm. The Black Beauty." I laugh and shake my head.

Sue, ever the understanding humanitarian, the Good Samaritan, amusingly stated, "Then you better get going. That's your calling, Dr. Love." I laughed and saw a twinkle in her sleepy eyes—a *Black Leprechaun* with the *Luck of the Irish*. It can't get any better!

A quick washup—teeth brushed, waste flushed, good to go! I was spiritually refreshed and out the door! It took me roughly an hour to drive from Boston down to Coventry, Rhode Island. I arrived with beer, champagne, knickknacks, polly wollies and do dahs. You were standing on the porch as I pulled up, and you had the look kids have the first time they see Santa Claus or Mickey Mouse. You helped me take in the goodies, and if I'm not mistaken, I had a little recorder or tape deck. I know this much. We had music, candlelight, wine, and roses. The *love of brotherhood* in full bloom and a pocket full of posies!

Then come those solemn moments, like ceremonies, not to be ignored, as was the case with your final departure from Coventry and the veterinarian establishment. This final moment, as fate would ordain, was punctuated with a cameo appearance by both your parents. What a way to close another glorious chapter of *The Way We Were!* But as Sam Cooke once sang, "A change gonna' come . . ." a new direction was being born.

It was more like the *larva-becoming-a-butterfly* scenario. Even better, the subtlety of boyhood into manhood. The severing of the umbilical cord. The catalyst for this transformation was my entrance. The stage was set. Oh! This was grand! The final curtain of this ever so realistic play of life—real to REAL! A living testimony. A performance truly lived and documented. ***It is written . . .*** But first, it must be lived!

Living theater—the circle of life. A true confession of love. *Destiny,* the play. Nothing is scripted, although heavily influenced by the natural character traits of the players. It's well rehearsed.

So there we were, in the last scene of the Closure. The final act of this episodic saga between J. Michael Sullivan and Mick E. The ever evolving story of love because that's what we were created for. Being a firsthand witness by our deeds. This is the known, not a norm.

Suddenly, it was time for you to move on . . . *depart!* The coming of *the Change.* The future always ***In the Moment.*** Its the conquest and its downfall. It's whatever is to be achieved and accomplished—or not. It's the full monty. Joy and glory mixed with sadness and disappointment, then sprinkled with numerous stumbling blocks. The haughty self-destruction. The fall that precedes the *fall of pride.*

On the good ship *Lollipop,* however, it is how pride is diminished that enables us to appreciate the art of humbleness. Going through the fire, so to speak, and the fire was about to heat up.

It was the end of a very warm and pleasant summer, and autumn was showing her colors as the leaves began to burn red in the chill of the night. You were close to returning to the core of your origin. The womb of your psychic being. The thing that can cloud one's own authentic self. One's culture. Church and sad state biologically disguised as our ethnicity. They can have a mighty hold on us. Especially, if you're proud of it or have fear of it. Unfortunately, for many, it's a mixed bag. Perhaps this is the reason and purpose of *the born again* principle. To set us free. Interesting, huh?

Nevertheless, it was summer's end, and fall was fast approaching. Your mom and pops were in da' house. It would be the second and last time I would engage your *daddy*—Frank Sullivan. It was a *com*-front-ment and **not** a *con*-frontation. I don't have to explain this to you. After all, you were there. A witness to the truth of that statement. A delicate moment. In the circles of life, always *the Revelation*. Departure is such sweet sorrow; hence, the present is always the future. Not tomorrow. For tomorrow isn't guaranteed or promised. This is why you must *keep hope alive—to keep da' faith!*

As I said, *Mom and Pops*—the Sullivans—were n' da' house with their only son. And you were the last! A Johnny-come-lately, having the same affect as when *Mary had a little lamb*. Wasn't the doctor surprised!

Surprised or not, you were the last of the Mohicans. Born after five beautiful daughters—Barbra, Margot, Carol-Noelle, my wife Sue, and Fran *(the maternal twins)*, **and** last but not least, you—**J. Michael**. How sweet it is! A late baby boomer.

Yes! You were the prime reason Mom and Pops were here. Here! To return you to your **roots** in Greenwich, Connecticut, where Irish eyes are said to be a-smilin'! This farewell, your swan song and return to your **roots**, wasn't necessarily indicative of *the Luck of the Irish*. I quickly became aware of this as soon as I came through the door connecting the hospital to the house. My exhilarating starlike entrance broke the silence, especially after I declared, "A family that packs together stays together." You'll have to admit that was da' Bomb! ***Bo-o-m!*** For me, it conjured up a picture of what it must've been like when God spoke, **"Let there be light!"** and created the sound barrier. This justifies the **golden** in "Silence is Golden." Validating the notion that a picture can be worth a thousand words. Silent pictures. No sound effects. Therefore, "Faith comes by hearing." Can you hear me now?

All that was left for me now were lights and camera. The rest is documented history. A divine moment in the circle of life. ***In the Moment, It is written . . .*** divine design—our love, a personal relationship with *Our Father.*

Sitting here writing, I can still see your *mom and pops* doing a five-star double take. It was classic! There are no Oscars for this. Why? It's too real. And this was not Hollywood. No! It was Coventry, Rhode Island. The real deal. Real to real. Rated X-cellent. True love. A gift.

After the double take, Mom went right into her *Fred Sanford* impersonation. This was the big one! She had one hand on her heart, the other raised to God. She was stunned. She couldn't say "Hail Mary" or "Hell no!" She couldn't even mutter out, **"It's him!** Jesus Christ." All she could do was to start cleaning. Cleaning everything, and she *whistled* while she worked! This scene was better than the Three Stooges, the Marx Brothers, or Charlie Chaplin. This was *black-and-white comedy.* The classics. Amos 'n' Andy.

Meanwhile you were packing some slacks into your suitcase when Pop Sullivan bellowed in a strong authoritarian voice, "Throw those things out!" A cloud of smoke rose above his head; his words regurgitated out of his mouth—being he was tightlipped and lockjawed--his voice bore a sharp low edge. Once said, he was triumphant in his decree. With a penetrating look, he glanced at your suitcase, then he took a gulp of beer relishing his victory—*father over son!*

I carefully watched you as the words hit your ears, permeating your soul, mind, and spirit. Your reaction was like that of someone who had been coldcocked or suckah' punched. Your eyes appeared glazed, the look a fighter has when he's gotten his bell rung. ***Bong!*** You were embarrassed, humiliated, and stunned. This was traumatic. Dare I say . . . devastating?

I can still recall the tone of your voice. You were thunderstruck, demoralized, uncertain, and your response was almost cowardly, as you replied, "Dad, I like these pants." That wasn't the right response. It smacked of insurrection. Even though weak, it was meek. *Blessed are the meek . . .*

Pop Sullivan narrowed his eyes and methodically pulled his pipe out of his mouth. His fixed stare marked the severity of the moment. This is official! He sat looking at you. Much as if he were a judge about to deliver a stiff sentence of *life or death. Pop* Sullivan: *the Hanging Judge!* A law all unto himself. A sovereignty of power and position. Final point. You were **HIS** son. Case! Therefore, he spoke in absolutes: "Throw those pants . . . out!" That was it! Case closed. ***Bang!*** The gavel's gravel. Monarchy rules. It's the law. This was official! A command, not a request! The Wizard of Oz had spoken, "Dorothy! *Ain't it som'thn'?*"

Understanding the verdict that was rendered, you walked toward the door, pants in hand. As you were about to pass your father, you stopped, your eyes met his. Eying one another in an *unbalanced* moment in the father/son relationship—a defining moment or, more to the point, a *re-finding* moment of Boyz II Men—because the Father and Son are One.

There you were in a dilemma, as if you were a little boy in *No Man's Land.* You had a pitiful look on your face. The look of a child who wants to have something that is dear to them, and for whatever the reason, the parent doesn't care to see the connection. For the parent, it's not about connecting—it's about domination, who's in charge, in control. In other words, *little person*, you're a child! We are god!

Suddenly, this wasn't Laurel and Hardy or Ma and Pa Kettle. It was *One Flew Over the Cuckoo's Nest!* This was high drama, and ironically, it was *High Noon!*

The plot thickens, intersecting the crossroads of life. *Manhood*—evolving in the psyche of the cycle of parental repetition—a psychotic break. An unexpected twist in the circle of life. The subtext: Always manifested under positive stress, which proves *love* is really blind—like faith!

For you, it was literally about the ability to draw the line . . . the boundary of your manhood rather than honorably crossing it. On the other hand, for *Pop* Sullivan, it was *time* to yield to the process and respect the line of demarcation. To abdicate and let go so a good man and a wonderful son can grow. This is my take. My point of view.

We all stood, frozen, **In the Moment** of truth. Now quiet and stilted, it had become a *Mexican standoff,* only to be interrupted by a simple question from me, "You do like those pants, don't you?" You nodded your head affirmatively. Continuing, I said, "Well, the pants are yours. You worked and paid for them. With all due respect to your father, keep them!"

Whoa! Time stopped. You stood and weighed your options. *Pop* Sullivan was drawn to the edge of his seat, waiting like a gallant warrior for the bell to continue doing battle.

You initiated the action. You threw me a look, then fired one to your father and smiled. It wasn't a smile of defiance; it was one of respect—for yourself! Self-assurance, self-recognition, and self-worth. Then you turned and walked back and placed the pants in your suitcase. Closing and locking it in triumph. Your manhood *ACQUITTED!* Case truly dismissed.

As you and Mom Sullivan—*queen mother*—got into the car, *Pop* Sullivan and I stood on the back porch, making yet another stand. This time, it was very **on** and **In the Moment**. We stood in silence, searching for that opening—that crack which would allow the son to shine in and release you to whom you'd become. An opening appeared in the reflection of a tear welling up from his beautiful soft-blue eyes. I realized my soul was seeing beyond the circumstance and illuminating me with wonder at God's perfection.

Speaking in a low, soft, humble, monolithic, apologetic manner, barely above a whisper, he sounded so precious, warm, and sweetly sincere. Resting his massive body on his cane, stately and most dignified, royalty is like that, he said, "Mick E. I want to thank you for being good to my daughter, whom I adore and treasure and thank you for watching over my son, who I dearly love. You're a good man. Thank you, Mr. Jones."

Re-recalling that cycle in the circle that parallels these events, shared by the constituents—the participants—all of which we circumnavigated as though it were on the rim of *life and death*, as in the beginning! **Rest in peace**, *Mom* and *Pop* Sullivan, *with much love!*

Parenthood, the framework of a child's social and spiritual consciousness, its basic awareness again *as in the beginning*. We shared many beginnings in the never-ending story of our lives. **Shared . . .** that which defined our spirit *In the Moment*, so to speak. Exciting, intriguing, loving, and blissful moments of soul bearing, stripped naked—literally. It's the truth. I love the naked truth. The truth uncovered. It's disarming, devoid of concealment. No deceit—it's Owego, New York.

O-we-go, and we did! There we were in Owego at my grandmother's home—Lelia Finley *a.k.a.* Mama Lelia. My father's mother, who immortalized this phrase, "Live while you can and die when you can't help it!" She was a grand dame, much like yo' mama—*a queen!*

Well, there we were in *the Big O!* There with Sue, Nia, and her husband of the time. George Terry, an affable human being. *Bye, George . . .*

You'd come down from Ithica, New York, where you were attending Elmira College. Now by invitation, you were in O-we-go at 67 Fox Street. Looking back in time and space, you had a standing invitation to everything Sue and I went to. *You were family, not* an *in-law!* You were and still are *our brother.* Inclusion is what the spiritual family is all about. It's a universal principle—*family. Our Father's* will being done. By grace, through the law. It's love.

There we were in Owego. It was another Hallmark-type setting. Quaint, rustic, antiquish. The grand dame—a work of art! Rich in old family values. **In the Moment!** Mama Lelia.

In this poetic, romantic, and enchanting environment of *love*—talking and dining by candlelight together with a little wine; a moonlight walk . . . *does it get any better?* Yes, the after-dinner smoke, a peaceful high of *love.* Wrapped up with a bubble bath . . . a cleansing. Finally, the closer, a *good-night hug.* An act of appreciation made in brotherly love. A big bear hug from Grizzly Adams! That's what you reminded me of back in the day when *truth and love* equaled a romantic memory of *love* because . . .

> *Hatred stirs up strife,*
> *But love covers all sins.*
>
> Proverbs 10:12

Ah . . . New York, New York. In the city you came. Yeah! You came to hang out with me and Sister Nia. Nia and I were there doing another journey of life. Canvassing. *Spiritual painting*—the art of designing fond spiritual memories from the experience. The lesson—a true confession of the essence of *love* when lived by grace.

The reason, on the surface, that Nia and I were in New York, New York, was that Nia was considering her options to work with the United Nations or some other diplomatic post. She is a linguist. She speaks several languages. She speaks in *tongues*. Mostly, she prophesies *love, truth, and the spirit*. Too real for politics of church and state of the *pull-pit* union of Satan. No love, just the letter of the law, which can be deadly in the wrong hands. Comin' out of the wrong mouths. No peace. No justice. No gas. No water. God's laws aborted, then cloned. A dead state of America—the Un-United! Hitler lives—9/11, do you hear me now? The enemy is always within! It's a dead issue son. The fall from Grace.

As for me, New York was hopefully helping me develop my **lounge act.** And you were searching desperately for yourself. A class act. Even then, I sensed a New York void. You didn't talk as much, which said volumes. There was a sadness in your eyes. They weren't smiling. That little spark, the glint was gone. That's when I realized you were a brilliant child. The core and foundation of us all. You were clever—not deceitful. Just spiritually retarded and *home alone!* In that summation or, more precisely, from it, I fully understood the fall of Rome. The fall from grace and why

King Kong fell. For real *love,* you got to survive your own hell. You must confess! You must tell!

In the Moment, I understood a New York minute! This is way before *9/11.* The World Trade Center was still trading. I was Dow Jones. There was stock in our brotherly love; that is until I researched your eyes. They revealed that the *market of love* was about to take a serious dip. This was the canvas on which this portion of the circle of life was painted in broad strokes. These brush strokes of *love* were painted for you and me. Because you are somebody painted firmly in my memory. Never to be forgotten nor forsaken. You're special! A gift. *Thank you!* Therefore, ***It is written . . .***

Greet one another with a holy kiss.

Romans 16:16

I charge you by the Lord that this epistle be read to all the holy brethrens. Greet all the brethren with a holy kiss.

2 Thessalonians 26:27

In the final return from then to now, it's all been a very enlightening experience. The journey. Culminating somewhat amusingly in New York. The Big Apple. It was after a very delicious breakfast prior to your leaving. You were low-key, almost mute. The only discussion radiated from your eyes, and they said, "Thank you. Much love." But they suppressed the good-byes or so long! Then you kissed me. Gave me thirty dollars and walked out, softly shutting the door behind you. You never could say good-bye! It was the door of symbolism and a metaphoric reality. A mystical mystique of understanding Judas and Jesus. Cain and Able. Liberals and conservatives. Gays and so-called straights. Religion and God. DNA and culture. Church and state. Ben-A-Dick Arnold. Schwarz-a-Neg-gah! Nero's fiddling as Rome burned. The Pope is well, but the priest ain't confessing nut'n! *Hail Mary.* Pee-wee Her-man. Satan's a drag queen!

Does that feel and sound like doom and gloom? By the light of the silvery moon, but don't fret for **us**. Hope is still alive, and the brotherhood breathes. *Kissie, kissie!*

February 4, 2006. It was Sue's—*our sister* and my wife—birthday. The proof to the spiritual psychic cycle. The circle of life was fulfilled. It was a mail thang. The simplicity of love. It arrived in a birthday postage for Sue from you. A collage of *the Salem Sullivans.* Clare, Kile, Connor, and you. A picture is worth a thousand words of *I love you!*

You actually spelled it out with the written expression thusly stated in the open space you had left to write "Happy Birthday to you, Sue. Here are some memories from 2005. The Salem Sullivans . . . a collage of your family's love."

It was read and viewed by me—the collage of the Salem Sullivan's—my family too! You knew that when you sent it! Like I said, "You're clever. Not deceitful. You're a good man." That's the only reason you're *my brotha' love.*

Tying up everything, I have thought and reflected about from then until now . . .

Much Love,
Yo' Brotha' Hu-Man!
Thanks 4 da' memories

WHAT IS CHRISTIANITY . . . 4-REAL?

I love proposing . . . questions. It's like an engagement. To make an offer. A proposal like marriage. You pop the question! You look for a response . . . the answer! Oh, I love getting answers, especially when I don't have a clue as to the question. Even if I did ask it. It's still the Q and As of life. In their equality of consciousness. The answer always evenly reflects the question, taking it to the next level. Higher consciousness. I believe it's all spiritually led by *Our Father*. God's will giving birth to the power of understanding the Qs and As of life. Being *born-again,* we then become humane in our understanding of why God, *Our Father,* gave birth to us. I'll tell you. It is to be *BORN AGAIN!* To love. I love it. Can you feel the love?

I question why I want to love. Why? The answer is *I need to love,* period! I hope it's perfectly clear. I understand my Qs and As! Love, that's it. That's what I was *born again* to do. Love, it's the law. I love the law. Mostly the lawgiver. My mother, my father, my God who governs and regulates humanity by the laws of its holy love. A universal command spoken in order for a human to be humane. Now. Here's the interesting part, and what I am about to say is mind boggling, to say the least. Hold your breath and get ready to sit down. If you are already down, you gonna pop up! and breathe! Here I go. To be humane, one must be **IN-SANE**. Can you wrap your amoeba mind around that? I couldn't, at first. It really made me appreciate . . .

> *"For my thoughts are not your thoughts, nor are your ways my ways," says the Lord.*
>
> Isaiah 55:8

It's the irony of the Lord. *In-Sane (I-S . . . is!).* A prerequisite for a human to be hu-mane!

Let us explore, investigate, and spiritually analyze *In-Sane* as *Sanity* for the human species. Let us use the premise that, generally speaking, most folks are humane, however. According to the polls I have taken, the focus of the media is to gather *stress stats*. Most of us—and damn near all of us—are walking around stressed and depressed, and this is being suppressed-, covered with a lot of positive thinking nonsense. Mumbling to ourselves, "It's all good!" However, inwardly, we're more up in the air and tied tighter than *Dick Cheney's* hatband. We're talking *bullshit!* Outwardly smiling with a *stiff upper lip*, meanwhile we're in THE X-treme reality. We're walking time bombs!

Spiritual nitroglycerin. Proving 911 is a spiritual deficiency. A combustible emotional psychological mental mess, like myself, ALL fall! We are in denial and off-balance. Highly dysfunctional, yet we call this *normal!* My ba-ad is all good.

I confess, we need help! Wouldn't you agree? We need spiritual surgery. A spiritual transformation—a transplant giving us a *renewed* mind. We need a doctor of the truth and spirit to operate immediately, if not sooner. *ASAP!* I am talking *ER. Scrubs.*

Here's the plot. This ain't *General Hospital, The Edge of Night,* or *As The World Turns* on its falling Wall Street ass-sets. I'm talking cure. Truth! Sanity. It's a loving spirit. A stimulus package of God's love. The *Saving Grace,* salvation, a gift of God's sanity. God's love and forgiveness. The cure and the healing!

Therefore, think of God's sanity as *the hospital.* Here, at *sanity hospital,* we can get serious spiritual help. Helping us with the balance of life, which is always in question. Sanity, something like HIP was to the *In Crowd* of the '60s, and now, fifty years later, sanity is at the HEART of the *In-Sane Crowd!*

In this *sane* setting, we erase all the problems because they're not allowed to exist here where the In-Sane becomes the In Crowd, and we, who embrace the "IN" of "Sanity," operate a very unusual hospital. No problem! It seems to be a great place 2 B-IN. Instead of Un-sane. No sanity at all! Zero tolerance for sanity! Which places man's definition of sanity into question. Is it IN or UN . . . Sane? This oxymoron mirrors UN-conditional love or CON-ditional love or another spiritual paradox—the answer to the art of proposing questions.

It establishes the purpose, the bottom line to my *sane* point, I love the *art of proposal* I confess. Proposal is not merely a question but an action. Proposing is an invitation. A marriage proposal is the precursor to participating in a union, which gives birth to the purpose of the divine will. Through God's love, sanity to a child's spirit of love within—the answer without question. Spiritual matrimony, guess who's the bride and who's the bride groom I ask?

I'm the inquisitive type by birth. It's my *born-again* nature. Seeking my purpose, to discern and to detect with senses other than sight. Walking by faith, asking God to guide me with an unbiased heart, when questioning man's concept of any and all things, specifically, things of *God—the Mother, the Father,* regarding their only begotten Son, Christ Jesus, and the Word, as it was in the beginning: *the truth!* This is very delicate for my eternal life because my salvation isn't to be toyed with! It's an event of such magnitude that to trust it to man's self-motivated explanations, interpretations, an opinionation is careless . . . IN-deed!

This is why man, self included, scripturally speaking, must always be questioned in and through the spirit of love. It's through God's loving, sensitive, sensible spirit will I sit still and be quiet. I retreat and go into my closet to meditate on and in the Word, privately asking God *Our Mother and Our Father* to clarify the issue. *(Please, please!*

Good God! It's obvious I'm in the book of James . . . *Brown!*
I feel . . . good! Good God!)

Seriously, I sit obediently in my closet, all cute and
cuddly, asking God, "Mommy, Daddy, you know I'm
your retarded, fallen, and confessed sinner, yo' child. I'm a
nasty, filthy rag. I've been called a San Francisco hag and a
Forty-second Street fag. Like the Apostle Paul, I'm a saved
wretch. No brag! I come to you in full armor, truth, and
in the spirit of your forgiving love. By grace, I humbly
ask for your assistance in this questionable examination of
man—self included. I beseech you to give me the insight,
the inspiration, and the strength of your love. The power
I need so I can thrust the sword of your truth and cut into
and spiritually dissect man's thinking on the word away
from your revealed thoughts through the Word. I ask
in faith, Is man in line? And is his alignment with you? I
know he's online—an Internet man—using the iPod,
downloading and down low! But is man a fisherman of
men . . . for you? For we all fall, even the Elected without
truth—the whole truth. So help us God! Without you,
man is just a man, lost in Myspace. A political state of his
degenerate mind. A sad place for the church when my **bad**
is **good!** Makes me question and wonder why man is going
under. He's so close to the edge. Is this the sign of man's last
days. Prayerfully and lovingly, I pose the question.

In the Moment, I sit quietly in the closet of my
self-imposed inquisitiveness. Undisturbed, unperturbed, I
commence to snap'n my fingers and patt'n my feet. All cute

and cuddly. In awe of God—*My Father! My Mother!* Secure and comfortable in this conversion.

I'm a confessed child of God. By grace. Let no one boast. It's a gift. Childhood! For children are the hook up to the Holy Spirit, dearly beloved! Children are important.

For God, children are God's delight. They are God's reflection. God's treasure. The salt of the earth, the flavor buds. God's divine seasoning: the children. The foundation of heaven, here on earth! *Born-again* family. God's children. The *peace bearers* of love--God, *Our Father, the* nurturer is Mother God's nature. This is why you don't fool with Mother God's nature—it disturbs fatherhood—and there goes the neighborhood! My children, undernourished and forsaken, have become the children of the damned, conformed to the world but not converted and having no humility.

Remember, Jesus said,

> *Assuredly, I say to you, unless you are converted and become as little children, you will by no means enter this kingdom of heaven. Therefore whoever humbles himself as this little child is the greatest in the kingdom of heaven.*
>
> Matthew 18:3-4

Then Jesus went further, taking a child in his arms, saying,

*Whoever receives one of these little children in my
name receives me; and whoever receives me, receives
not me but him who sent me.*

Mark 9:37

And what about this one . . .

*Train up a child in the way he should go, and when
he is old he will not depart from it.*

Proverbs 22:6

Well, my beloved, truth has no age. At seventy-one,
I return with conviction to my original conclusion. *It's
hamma' time! Obama time!* Now I will hit the *nail* on its
head. It's the elected *Million Dollar Man March* question
time.

Come on, get real 'n tell me, are *so-called* Christians
the *real deal*? Do they truly represent Christ, or have they
become like crystals, dazzling the eye without heart. Or
are they fluid, as is *the light--the truth* and *the way*? The
go-through door to God, *Our Father,* who conceived the
immaculate birth of salvation? Peace on earth! Jesus . . .
the *truth*, the fulfillment of God's forgiving love. The
resurrected In-Sane forgiveness of *physician heal thyself* love?
Now we, you, and me are in *the hospital* of the sane, *born
again* of sound mind, renewed in Christ with the power,
the gift of discernment by grace, let no one boast of our
discharge!

Thereby, returning to my question of discernment, are these *so-called Christians 4 real and 4 Christ,* or are they mere foreplay? Are they just pious world religious schismatic of Christianity? Modern day Pharisees and Sadducees? Ruling with seductive pleasure, like their forefathers, using their tradition of self-imposed doctrine to justify their selfish, greedy, sexually carnal addictions, and perverted behavior, all the while praising God? Inwardly, they're ravenous vampires, wolves in sheep's clothing! Spiritual turncoats. False prophets. Spiritual infiltrators. To me, a Judas and Benedict Arnold *4 sure!* Religious terrorists! ***It is written . . .***

> *For we do not wrestle against flesh and blood, but against principalities, against powers, against the rulers of the darkness of this age, against spiritual hosts of wickedness in the heavenly places.*
>
> Ephesians 6:12

Free at last to ask!

Nevertheless, I'll let God, *Our Father,* of mercy—the just God be the judge. I'll get my biased out of the way. For I, like all others, am fallen and will eventually find myself, one day, standing before God in judgment. On that fateful day, I will be standing with my lawyer and petitioner, **Christ Jesus**, the resurrected and the grace of my salvation. A gift of love. Redeemed and represented.

I can just imagine Judgment Day. On that day, as Gabriel blows his horn *beep beep!* Peter, the *Rock, will be rockin',* rollin', and screamin' like Elvis, "Hear, hear! Like faith, it comes by hearing. Now hear this: Court is in session. All the fallen rise. The Honorable God, Our Father, presiding. All sit!" After all the Fallen settle down, the Rock continues, "Note, there will be no swearing on the Bible, for it is a blaspheme of religious behavior; high treason to the will according to the Scriptures! Just say yea or nay. Again, you have heard that it was said to those of old that you shall not swear falsely, but shall perform your oaths to the Lord. But I say to you, do not swear at all, neither by heaven for it is God's throne; nor by earth for it is his footstool; nor by Jerusalem for it is the city of the great king."

It is written . . .

As I live, says the Lord,
Every knee shall bow to me,
And every tongue shall confess to God.

Romans 14:11

Nor shall you swear by your head, because you cannot make one hair white or black. But let your "Yes" be "Yes," and your "No," "No." For whatever is more than these is from the evil one.

Matthew 5:36-37

Therefore, based on the aforementioned, I must ask hard questions in and through the spirit. Prodding myself with the only truth—in God, *Our Father,* trusting not man, self included, but relying on scriptural prophesy. ***It is written . . .***

> *Take heed that no one deceives you. For many will come in my name, saying, "I am the Christ," and will deceive many.*
>
> Matthew 24:4-5

Deceivers coming in the name . . . Halloween, Hollywood, *so-called* Christians of the world church and sad state duped into religious self-righteousness. A politically correct mask. A charade that preaches *UN*-conditional love. The spirit of the *UN*-christ, which raises the Ante from just a bet to *ANTI!* In high and low places validating my *Million Dollar Man March* question: **What is a Christian 4-Real?**

Are these *so-called Christians* the real deal 4-Christ? Or simply a fraudulent, fanatical, hyped up, misled, religious, and pious schismatic group of *wannabes*?

In the Moment and at the juncture of my validation by Scripture, I question world religion's *so-called Christian.* In particular, let's call it a crosscheck. *Praise da' Lord!*

The **CROSS,** the core symbol of Christ's deity, his ultimate expression of eternal love and compassion compels a true follower of Christ to seek out the scriptures, asking, "How do Christians—no, not how—but why do Christians become Christians?" Jesus was not a Christian.

I never recall reading anywhere in Scriptures where Jesus said he wanted to be a Christian. As it was, he was at odds with those men for whom religion overshadowed God's true word, becoming a weapon of administration, power, and control. They sought to elevate *their* interpretation of the law to that of the Word as given to Moses and the prophets. Jesus saw through them and *their law* and erased it by giving us **two** greater *commandments* from which should hang all the law of the prophets. Thus, he washed his hands, and the hands of all mankind, of the mess created by a corrupt and perverted leadership—church and sad state, principality of a demonic one world government. Blasphemy. The anti Christ world government.

Jesus respected the law as given to Moses, to Isaiah and declared by John the Baptist and other prophets who had laid the foundation of his coming. He consistently rearranged the way men were to think as to the propriety of religion and the law.

Among other things, it was the commerce of religion that Jesus found spiritually bankrupt—like the economy. Dead! Jesus made himself abundantly clear on numerous occasions that one should render what is Caesar's to Caesar and what is God's to God, *Our Father.* Religion traffics in suffering. Jesus came not to condemn but to save the world. Thus, he set out on his ministry to teach why religion, as it existed then and still exists to this day, is not of *Our Father* but of man! Jesus came to save us, to redeem us, and to purchase back our soul from Satan. Our very soul, which was forfeited in the Garden of Eden. Yet though redeemed on the cross by his death and resurrection, Satan pursues the hearts of fools into reclaiming this folly through *so-called* religion and in the name of *Christianity*. Here's what Scripture says about religion,

> *If anyone among you thinks he is religious, and does not bridle his tongue but deceives his own heart, this one's religion is useless. Pure and undefiled religion before God and the Father is this: to visit orphans and widows in their trouble, and to keep oneself unspotted from the world.*
>
> James 1:26-27

See, religion is over and Christianity, in particular, is more spotted than a litter of Dalmatians, and its purity is as stained as its Crystal Cathedral stained-glass windows. Religious people cannot bridle their tongues. They are too busy laying hands on little boys and little girls, your wife or your husband, yo' dog! This is religious church and the sad state of religious people are the reason the law has fallen into the streets of depression.

People religiously lusting after money, the greedy over the needy, taxing, and tithing, but not abiding, still with the audacity to come in the name, singing "We Are the World." *Blasphemy.* This is what Jesus came to save us from—the world's religions. *Blasphemy!* Christianity, in particular!

All of the world religions are world government approved. This is why you can't separate church from state. The religious line blurs and overlaps. Always mixing and mingling.

Strange bedfellow is this church and state business 'cause ain't nobody straight. So same sex marriage, it has government appeal. It has already been approved. It's the world and what could be more worldly than world religion—it's licensed by a world government that religion blesses. How *chummy!* Sexually active praisin' da' Lord!

Jesus's primary purpose was to establish a relationship between heaven and earth. To separate light from dark, not to anoint world religion.

> *These things I have spoken to you, that in Me you may have peace. In the world you will have tribulation; but be of good cheer, I have overcome the world.*
>
> John 16:33

See there? This is Jesus talking! He says he has **overcome the world!** He has it in the bag. It is a **done deal**—no need to wonder if it's the real deal. This is signed, sealed, and delivered! Since this is a "done deal," the fact that the church and state, which so proudly declares they are financing the resolution to this thorny issue with taxes and tithes and offerings. It's always about the money. Listen up, you devoted, patriotic Americans! Devotion is tied to even *the Elect—money, money!* And Jesus laid it bare, yet *without eyes to see or ears to hear,* we continue to finance Satan in his pursuit of destruction. The unbalanced can't balance the budget. They never will 'cause they don't have the will in the first place.

No one can serve two masters; for either he will hate
the one and love the other, or else he will be loyal to
the one and despise the other. You cannot serve God
and mammon.

Matthew 6:24

Yeah! It's about the **Kingdom** and not the money. Money rests at the root of evil. In and of itself, money will do nothing but clutter the stage; but in the hand of man, money can and usually is the root of evil.

For the love of money is a root of all kinds of evil,
for which some have strayed from the faith in their
greediness, and pierced themselves through with many
sorrows.

1 Timothy 6:10

Let's back up and really put the *nail* in the crosshairs of our reality check.

Now godliness with contentment is great gain. For we
brought nothing into this world, and it is certain we
can carry nothing out. And having food and clothing,
with these we shall be content. But those who desire
to be rich fall into temptation and a snare, and into
many foolish and harmful lusts which drown men in
destruction and perdition.

1 Timothy 6:6-9

This is serious pride. Like Wall Street and world church and state government in which pride goes before the haughty fall . . . and all fall, self included. I am by grace, saved! I confess! *Will you?* Hear me Bernie Madoff. *U-Ponzi!*

I confess Jesus. I receive him. So I can receive the Sender. The one who sent Jesus, and Jesus prefaced this opportunity to receive the Sender with "*whosoever.*"

For the legalist, Jesus never said the reception of him would make you Christian or a Jew! Back in the day, talking to the Jews and Gentiles who believed on him, he said,

> *If you abide in my word, you are my disciples indeed.*
> *And you shall know the truth, and the truth shall*
> *make you free.*

John 8:31-32

Therefore, beloved, in freedom I ask, **"What is a Christian . . . 4-Real?"** By their deeds? The actions of their Christian expression is division. Is Christ divided? It's the confusion of the church and state.

> *For God is not the author of confusion but of peace,*
> *as in all the churches of the saints.*

1 Corinthians 14:33

I mean, how do Christians become *Ku Klux Klan Kristians?* I guess that's UN-conditional, UN-sane love. *Konflict and konfrontation.* I guess it's *klan destiny* . . . a well-kept secret of *Kristianity*. Unrighteous wars. No peace. Never justice. This seems to put light on why sex is unwed and violent and very dark. Leaving God's children raped, molested, and abused in churches, temples, synagogues, and mosques, and people can't figure out why *so-called* homosexuals are ruling. I'll tell you why. They know what religious people know. *So-called* Christians in particular. Even the Mafia has got a *homosexual hit squad*. It's the UN-conditional love—the kiss of death. Very taxing!

Homosexuals aren't gay. They are like the KKK—*out of the closet*. They're the people. Yeah, US . . . homies! Church and sad state is a culture of state-sponsored religious *candy strippers* ruling from the dark side with Christians, in particular, operating outside the box. Jack's off, out in the woods, all alone. There he meets up with the fox who makes him into Jill. The coup d'etat is sending him up the *hill* to the *well* with the *will* to bring back a pail full of money, honey. Both church and state are sadly very thirsty, having denied themselves the *Living Waters of eternal truth*.

It's politically correct and constitutionally sound, nevertheless, scripturally unsound. Un-found, and according to the Scriptures, we're to go into our room, a quiet place of prayer and shut the door.

> *But you, when you pray, go into your room, and when you have shut your door, pray to your Father who is in the secret place; and your Father who sees in secret will reward you openly.*
>
> Matthew 6:6

I believe this calls for two *SNAPS* and a *CIRCLE!* It's the truth! *Hail Mary and Esther knows Ruth!*

This is why I search the scriptures in spirit and in truth. And let the inspired Scriptures do what they were inspired to do—to *reproof.* Reburk!

> *All scripture is given by inspiration of God and profitable for doctrine, for reproof, for correction, for instruction in righteousness.*
>
> 2 Timothy 3:16

And the way you get instruction is through personal, up front and one-on-one communication with the Teacher!

> *And do not be called teachers; for One is your Teacher, the Christ.*
>
> Matthew 23:10

> *But seek first the kingdom of God and His righteousness, and all these things shall be added to you. Therefore do not worry about tomorrow, for tomorrow will worry about its own things. Sufficient for the day is its own trouble.*
>
> Matthew 6:33

I heard that! That is a zigzag—*SNAP!* Hear it? Did you hear that? Seek first the *Kingdom*—not the inspired book or religions. This is getting good. Remember . . .

*In the beginning was the Word, and the Word was
with God, and the Word was God.*

John 1:1

God, the Instructor, the Creator, the Inspirer of the
inspiration given to Scriptures. In the beginning, **he . . .**
*THE **WORD!** and not the book.*

*And the Word became flesh and dwelt among us, and
we beheld His glory, the glory as of the only begotten
of the Father, full of grace and truth.*

John 1:14

The proof to my point being the Kingdom first, not the
book. Secondary to seeking the Kingdom is the searching of
the inspired Scriptures, and when searching the scriptures,
first and foremost, be in the full armor God has provided
so as not to be deceived or led astray. In truth and spirit. In
God's love. Which governs the fruits that keep us *IN-Sane*,
not *UN*-sane.

*But the fruit of the Spirit is love, joy, peace,
longsuffering, kindness, goodness, faithfulness,
gentleness, self control. Against such there is no law.
And those who are Christ's have crucified the flesh
with its passions and desires. If we live in the Spirit, let
us also walk in the Spirit. Let us not become conceited,
provoking one another, envying one another.*

Galatians 5:22-26

This ain't judgment, these are the facts—the proof! And religion, my beloved, provokes and irritates and does not save you! Nor will it point you toward Christ or God. It will point **you 2 yourself.** This is the proof of the truth of the First Commandment God gave to the Hebrews upon leaving Egypt.

Have no other gods before you. Nothing. Not in the likeness of man, animal, or any creeping thing on the earth, nor of anything that lives in the waters. When **you** become the center of **your** life, **YOU** become the god—an *idol!* American or otherwise. Thereby arousing and provoking an In-Sane, jealous, and living God to anger and wrath. Leave your iPod at home and worship him and him alone through the person of Christ Jesus.

FYI. That's why he sent Jesus so we'd have an EXAMPLE *in the flesh* of what and how we should do what we should be doing and are not doing. I wonder why?

When straying, it allows followers to be manipulated, culturally entrapped in a world of dysfunctional, megalomaniacal religious maniacs wielding state-sponsored religious trademarks with complex tax shelters. Like a First Methodist, Baptist, Catholic, Jew, Muslim, Jehovah Witnesses, AND, would you believe, so-called Christians? And if you're a believer in Christianity, what IS Christianity's *faux pas*—4-Real? The original question, as in the beginning, is answered searching the Scriptures. For instance . . .

*. . . that if you confess with your mouth the Lord Jesus
and believe in your heart that God has raised Him
from the dead, you will be saved. For with the heart
one believes unto righteousness, and with the mouth
confession is made unto salvation.*

Romans 10:9-10

A shout-out 2 Jesus! Okay, my legalistic pundits, critics, and impatient naysayers—it's nitty-gritty time. For the record, my addicted church and sad state religious culturally indoctrinated traditionalist—**my** brothers and sisters—and that includes my bi/trigender in high and low places, com' on out and join me in a family discussion.

Let's break the bonds of We Are the World—the confused, confounded, confabulated, and entrapped people drowning in a cesspool of culturally, politicized world church and sad state running amok with lustful, sadistic pedophiles! *SNAP! CRACKLE! POP!* That thang! What ev'va yo' thang is? It's nasty! Especially, my beloved Christians in particular. Yo' flock . . . confused and divided.

My question and focal point to the religious family to the sheep who can hear and Christians, in particular, is that **my** light **is** on you! It shines bright. It's the love of the truth—a reflection. You claim to be *so* there! In light of that, I propose to the delegates of Christians following the light, please tell me and show me where does it say in Romans 10:9-10 that you or I have to be a Christian or anything else? I'm not saying you can't be one or another or som'em else. *SNAP! SNAP!* I'm splitting hairs here! I never saw the word "Christians" in Romans 10:9-10 that denoted anything except . . .

"Whosoever." Whoever! Whatever! This sounds like an "open door" policy. Come one, come all! Welcome to God! Through the Christ, the Door, the resurrected Jesus, who called to ALL because all fall short of the glory of God. Jews and Greek . . . *whosoever*! ALL, as it is with sin, is generic to God. *God is not a respecter of person.* Details change, but the principle stays the same. There is no distinction. It's all in the family to God. Ironically, family is the problem. His children, who Christians swear they are, will swear ON the Bible—the Book that so clearly states, "Do not swear," and you can't tell them they are wrong. They claim to know God personally. Scriptures refute that claim by saying . . .

> *He was in the world, and the world was made through him, and the world did not know him. He came to his own, and his own did not receive him. But as many as received him, to them he gave the right to become children of God, to those who believe in his name: who were born, not of blood, nor the will of the flesh, nor the will of man, but of God.*
>
> John 1:10-13

I got to stop and **shout, "Praise da' Lord!"** This is why God, in his infinite wisdom, left the door wide open to whoever is like Me and believes and calls on his name. His name which is above all others. They—whoever *they* are—will be saved! Whoever! Christians, Jews, Muslims,

Hindus, voodoos, gender benders—whoever! Epileptics, crippled blind midgets—whoever! It's an *open door*. **Knock!** Raise the hand and press the knuckles to the wood and knock! Welcome all. Come in and sup with *me—I AM the Lord!*

It would be simpler if Jesus wasn't the Christ; then this whole dysfunctional mess could be moved somewhere else, onto someone else and the blame outsourced to another culture entirely! But Jesus is *the Christ . . .* the living God! *What is a Christian . . . 4-Real?* Let's check scriptures, for *It is written . . .*

> *Then Barnabas departed for Tarsus to seek Saul. And when he had found him, he brought him to Antioch. So it was that for a whole year they assembled with the church and taught a great many people. And disciples were first called Christians in Antioch.*
>
> Acts 11:25-26

This was long after the *crucifixion of Jesus!* It's that Scripture right there! That one in particular, I question Christianity and all world religion church and state, but Christianity, in particular.

My contention is predicated on Acts 11:25-26. The disciples came to Antioch, and some men or some body began to call them *Christians.* By giving them credibility, they also gave tacit "authority" to men of the teachings as they spoke to those gathered in the churches. These disciples, who brought the assembly together to hear of the teachings of Jesus, became the focus of ignorance and unbelief. In an environment of hostility and enmity, *Christian* soon became a name reviled. This led to persecution, which the true believer was able to accept because of the faith instilled in their hearts after hearing of our Lord and Savior, Christ Jesus, who suffered the greatest of all when crucified on a tree, bloodied by the sword, and mocked by all who passed by. But the disciples knew that such a time of persecution was inevitable because Jesus himself said that we who would believe on him, who would speak his name and walk in his ways, would become the object of ridicule, torture, and even death. He warned us all of what lay ahead for the true believer until the time of his Second Coming.

Nevertheless, true believers who walk in faith with Christ, now two thousand years later, aren't so terribly different than the disciples who taught the assemblies in the churches of Antioch. Though scattered to the ends of the earth, Christ's followers today are cupbearers for Christ, the King of kings and Lord of lords. Christianity is an umbrella to shading a *people* who are dedicated to defining the teachings of Christ as **It is written** in the Holy Bible to persons *with ears to hear and eyes to see.*

Jesus advised an eager young man asking what he must do to be saved. Jesus told him to go home, sell all that he owned, and give the proceeds to the poor. Then he could return, pick up his cross, and follow him. Sadly, he said that was too much to ask.

Pleasures are passing; joy is eternal. The distinction is a matter of heart. Jesus knew he made an untenable offer to his eager aspirant. Today, many so-called Christians fail by expecting the best of both worlds without suffering the spiritual ascension needed to be free of fleshly bondage. This suffering was referred to by Jesus Christ as "If anyone desires to come after Me, let him deny himself, and take up his cross and follow Me. For whoever desires to save his life will lose it, but whoever loses his life for My sake will find it" (Matthew 16:24-25). *Our Father* has many tasks for the U.S. to perform, but they cannot be faithfully executed when toting a millstone around our neck. Many are called but few make the journey.

Today, I see that we're just as divided as those living in Antioch. Idols abound. The unbelievers scoff, ridicule, and persecute. The converts suffer terribly at the hands of the infidels. Satan opposes the conversion and salvation of the Muslim, the Hindi, the pagan of any stripe, and creates unbelievably harsh suffering.

The *so-called* Christian is a product of materialism. Satan uses *stuff* to attract and divide believers. The more one focuses on *stuff*, the less they focus on God, *Our Father.* They have become stylish replicas of the decadent Roman or Greek pagan. Satan cultivates men and women who preach the *feel good* antidote to discipline and suffering. He has set their social barometer on *warm and fuzzy.*

These *so-called* Christians are not embedded in the Word, nor do they want to be. As it was in Antioch, the defamed and desperate pagan priest sought every fiery dart available for wounding the *Christ-I-AM* teachers, yet sparing those who taught not the Word of Christ but a brand of their own—laced with lies, inaccuracies, and false promise.

The truth is, *whosoever* believes, confesses, and acknowledges the merciful act of crucifixion of God's only begotten Son and his resurrection for our restoration, redemption, and salvation has entered into a personal relationship and knows Christ Jesus as their personal Lord and Redeemer. The truth and spirit of God.

So-called Christians, in particular, are divided more than street cocaine, having allowed Satan to splinter their beliefs with state sponsored world religion. ***It is written . . .***

> *Is Christ divided? Was Paul crucified for you? Or were you baptized in the name of Paul?*
>
> 1 Corinthians 1:13

Paul taught immature young disciples the difference between man and deity. Paul thanks God, in the next verse, that he baptized none except two friends who understood the relationship. Among those who were unable to hear these words as they came from Paul, began to splinter away, preferring to sensationalize this individual or that one over Christ who had died in a land far off. Some men soaked up the light of fame furiously and others sought out watersheds of personal gain. Jesus Christ came to this world to save it and not condemn it, and he arrived at the zenith of corruption.

The work of Satan had begun to splinter as well. Working the world front and the heavenly front. He couldn't win two wars at once and was cast from heaven and God's presence for eternity. In anger and frustration, he began working at the local level—the mind of man and the relationship of himself to this world. Making friends with the world scripturally, a most dangerous engagement. And one Satan fosters.

In fact, he is the original foster parent program. Perhaps we could learn, but he has veiled his input incredibly well. Few daytime Christians are willing to dig deeply enough. To shine the light of truth into their own *his-terical* darkness.

It is "principality," which creates the vacuum for the falling of the spirit. The ruler of church and sad state with a stranglehold on *so-called* Christians. Walking by faith of world religion. Licensed by the sad state of world governments. *So-called* Christians proudly worshiping and idolizing, proudly singing "We Are the World." The dark knights of Satan's—no light, no salt.

> *Do you not know that friendship with the world is enmity with God? Whoever therefore wants to be a friend of the world makes himself an enemy of God.*
>
> James 4:4

And if Christians are the real deal, how can you hate, lust, kill, lie, steal, and be the world. You are to **overcome evil with good!** Your faith is to be bound in the light of the love for the Lord and his Word.

Let's go deeper. There are Muslims, Chinese—whoever—all over this planet converting like children to follow Christ and are being persecuted for Christ. Standing up on their faith for Christ's sake.

This suffering is beyond imagination, yet for the Muslim, Chinese—whoever—the brothers are steeped in their old ways. It will cleanse them and prepare them for the greatest experience of their life. The joy of being united with Christ—*without doubt*. Born-again. *Free at last!*

Every religious conformist has doubt. It's the confusion of sin—fear. UN-certainty. The UN-conditional love caused by religion's policy to divide and conquer. A cultivated world, political tradition lacking the spirit. The strength of God's love and fulfillment to be conformed, to be committed, and to raise the conscious awareness to support the Muslims, Chinese, or whoever—converted by the Spirit, born-again, those now openly suffering and being persecuted for Christ's sake. Each *whoever* or *whatever*—**ALL** literally dying for the sake of confessing Christ and not ashamed. Severe, maybe. Necessary, absolutely. Haunting, yes, but praiseworthy. *Praise da' Lord!*

They are standing on the word by faith, NOT by religion, world affiliates, principality, church, and state. One world government—the anti-Christ. The fulfillment of scriptures, the prophesy of *the false Christ* producing false Christians. Can I get an ***AMEN!***

You legalists can check Matthew 24:24 or 2 Peters 2:1-3. ***It is written . . .*** Ephesians 6:12.

The Word in the beginning: **God!** Our Mother/Father. Our friend. God called Abraham a friend, and many Muslims and Chinese count Abraham as a part of their lineage and for good reason. He came from the region we now call Iraq. Blood ties are there, and so much cleansing, weeding, suffering, sowing, loving, and growing to do before harvest. A friend they have in Abraham who **IS** a friend of God. Friends in high places. It always helps.

And scripture was fulfilled which says, "Abraham believed God, and it was accounted to him for righteousness." And he was called the friend of God.

James 2:23

A friend loves at all times, and a brother is born for adversity.

Proverbs 17:17

Our brothers and sisters who are boldly standing on the Word by faith—Muslims, Jews, Chinese, whoever—need to hear from believers. Muslim, Jews, Chinese converts are showing the true spirit of their commitment to confess Jesus as Lord and Savior. They are willing to lay their lives down.

Oh, what a friend we have in Jesus. And what friends and brothers we have in all those who have literally put their lives on the line for Christ's sake. Here's what Jesus said to this courageous and committed deed in and for his name's sake . . .

If anyone desires to come after me, let him deny himself, and take up his cross, and follow me. For whoever desires to save his life will lose it, but whoever loses his life for my sake will find it. For what profit is it to a man if he gains the whole world, and loses his own soul? Or what will a man give in exchange for his soul? For the Son of Man will come in the glory of his Father with his angels, and then he will reward each according to his works.

Matthew 16:24-27

And Muslims, Jews, Chinese, and mostly the *whoevers* are being more Christlike than *so-called* Christians. This is why I ask the question: **What is a Christian . . . 4-Real?** For Christ? It has nothing to do with being a *so-called* religious person, a Christian, in particular. It is—*Do you believe? Confess? Personally know? Trust and obey and do the will of God, Our Father, "and to love ye one another as I love you."*

This is a commandment spoken by Jesus who came for "whoever they" ALL are! Jesus, who laid his life down for ALL the *WHOEVERS* so that WHO-**SO**-EVER may come to know eternal life with *Our Father.*

Greater love has no one than this, than to lay down one's life for his friends. You are my friends if you do whatever I command you.

John 15:13-14

Owe no one anything except to love one another, for he who loves another has fulfilled the law.

Romans 13:8

What is a Christian . . . 4-Real? I really don't know. Is the answer to this question found when Jesus said,

Again I say to you that if two of you agree on earth concerning anything that they ask, it will be done for them by my Father in heaven. For where two or three are gathered together in my name, I am there in the midst of them.

Matthew 18:19-20

Therefore, whether Christian, Jewish, Muslim, Hindu, voodoo, or all those who do come together in the name . . . In love. In peace. In forgiveness. Like God, the Father and Mother. The spirit of truth. In his name, I honor and salute you and humbly serve you, my beloveds. For these are the conditions of love.

Mr. President

February 22, 2008

Dear Mr. President:

I use that salutation boldly and as a matter of fact, because by all real and practical standards, you are the President. You are *the change*. And . . . here you are: 'Mr. President, Your Honor.' You, *O'Bama da' Hamma* of change! The change *We The People* cry for. The change *Born Again*. A return to the *United States* and you are the vehicle—the vessel to that Union. A real, human change back to a reality *of the people, by the people and for the people.*

Unprecedented, Mr. President, you are the Phoenix raising us up from the ashes of discontent on the wings of change. Mr. President, you have become the harmonizing factor of true change. The only breath of fresh air to wash over the capital of this great nation since D.C. became a hotbed of Dysfunctional Christians reeking foul political air-rogance saturated with ill-will, war and tyranny.

Mr. President, you are the heart and soul of this *Change!* The spirit of true grit. You are politically correct, lovingly bold and everything about you is warm, genuine and ready for change. You simply ain't cold.

You're not liberal or conservative—nor left, right or White. You are the Whole. The change that Unites. You have an adorable mate, and a woman of considerable character, who, like you, is not a red, white or blue state. A united spiritual fate. Love never hates. As a result, the Eagle of change has appeared on the horizon of our political landscape. You are a man of true distinction.

Sir! You're pro-life and a servant of the people. The greatest. The People's Choice. So . . . *We The People* say "Let's Stay Together" for real change. You're the proof. *We The People* are the family God blessed when He Blessed America. It's Our Father's will. The *God We Trust* in for a United States of consciousness. For real change . . . *Oh, say can you see* . . . can you hear me now?

Therefore, Mr. President, congratulations!

Sincerely,
We The People
The Government *of the People, by the People and for the People*

I'M AUDACIOUS . . . THEE AUDACITY!

I'm Audacious . . . Thee Audacity! Just so you know that this is a Greek tragedy—an American history. This is real *shake-spiritual.* 'Cause it's from the heart of God's inspired will. Therefore, I'll write as Paul wrote to the Ephesians, to the Galatians, to young Pastor Timothy. I write to all . . . *whoever!* Nevertheless, my attention and words are focused precisely on the prime minister, *Mr. Barack Obama,* Mr. President again!

As in the beginning, *I'm audacious. I'm bold! Been called arrogant and rash! Marketed by originality and verve. In other words, "the audacity" an artistic reality to compose "all" I'm about to state. I'm a paradoxical oxymoron by grace . . . thee audacity.* A paradoxical oxymoron by grace. A conscientious reflection of the light. Therefore, I write in spirit and truth. My beloved brother, the president. The prime minister to the world. The ripple effect in the evolution of the cause. Now the change. Moving forward. Starting with yourself

"The Man in the Mirror". It's the plank and the speck principle in Matthew 7:5. And never forget, overlook or take light. You can't serve two masters in Luke 16:13. I read the money: *In God We Trust.* I also searched the Scriptures in regards to *change*. It's a divine attribute of *Our Father*. His will being done, not thine. It is change for us but a part of his unchanging plan.

> *And do not be conformed to this world but be transformed by the renewing of your mind, that you may prove what is good and acceptable and perfect will of God.*
>
> Romans 12:12

Minister Obama, God's faithful servant. An assistant of the universal God. In discipleship. The trust of God bestowed upon you. A trustee. One who is evolving, an intricate part of *Revelations.* The fulfillment of *prophecy—YOU!* Mr. President again!

It was in the twenty-first century. The year was two thousand and four—a day of our Lord. The prophecy was spoken, declared, and claimed. The revelation took place as I was doing my taxes without representation. An annual report. A tabulation of my accountability. To decide what is owed to Caesar, as opposed to what is from God, the one whom I trust and who has generously opened up heaven and rained his blessings upon me. This is an annual event: *the Feast of Discernment.* It is a day when everybody gathers together and is challenged to discern what is real and what is fantasy, what is truth and what is a lie, what gives and what takes! It's amusing to me, the more things change, the more they seem to remain the same. Da' Polotricks, a slight of hands.

Except on this night, it was subtle, but it became different as the night took on a distinctive air. An *awe* washed over me. It occurred simultaneously when my attention was drawn magnetically to the television. At first glance, I thought it was a cute impression of Mr. Potato Head I was viewing, until I heard the rush, really a *ROAR*. The words projected were carefully chosen with a powerful exhortation to stimulate the responses embedded into his message. **In the Moment** it was the circle of life. I was Mufasa, and this was Simba, but not in THIS reality. But rather it was the keynote speaker at the 2004 Democratic National Convention. A Boston irony, for it was here the first patriot for America's freedom was killed—for change—was **Crispus Attucks**, a black man. God bless America. A phrase stated often. The speaker was hypnotic! On fire!

I was transfixed. I became riveted to what I was seeing and hearing. There was this glow. This aura surrounding the speaker who had a boyish innocence. There was a twinkle, a light flashing within his eyes. They glistened. His lips were sensuous yet not seductive. They were perfectly shaped. They released his words. Shaping vowels and consonants into words which he articulated in such a way that they became *majestic!*

Striking deep in the core of my being quite mesmerizing. Stimulating a sensation that was raising my consciousness. I could feel my chest expanding, as though my spirit were being elevated, and I arose and walked right up to the TV. I stood in front of my wife, partially obstructing her view. She mused, *If you get any closer, you'll be on the podium with him!*

I recall standing there mesmerized. I kept asking myself, as if in a trance, who is this? I'll try to paraphrase what I believe he said.

I'm not talking red states, blue states, black, white, yellow, brown, purple, polka dot, gay, or never-straight states! I'm talking *the United States* . . . the US of A—US-A(LL). In the Universal God We Trust. Who made us by grace—united! For we are the world God so loved . . . loved us so much he gave us free will! We can choose our point of view or God's viewpoint. That's *pro choice!* Either point of view chosen. One or the other. Whichever there will be *change*—like I said and I believe, that's what he said.

I said, "That's deep!" Especially the way I said, "He said it!" This man had got som'em on his mind. It's heavy on his heart and busing loose. It's coming out of his spirit. It's universal love. It's in his DNA—change. It starts with inner peace. A human necessity. In order to move forward, I'm goin' *WOW, WOW.* That's an **Aha** moment! *In the Moment* epiphany. I turned to my precious wife. I say, "Sue. This is the next president of the United States. The prime minister to the world."

Everything about him was unique. Especially his name. Mr. Barack "Who's Sane!" Obama! A new beginning. A new dawn. A new His-Story! The following day, starting with the morning news, everything I had sensed and felt from the night before was being confirmed. Starting with the morning TV shows. The news. Political talk shows— everybody! Especially *Oprah!* It's a serious buzz. It's in the air. It's everywhere. You can feel the vibe. The air is charged about the senator from Chicago, Illinois. The o'vanight political superstar. Bright and shining. This buzz followed me all through the day. I went to the Hollywood YMCA. I'm in the men's locker room. I barely got my drawers dropped, and I hear *Obama!* This is the Hollywood YMCA, okay!

On the serious side of the prophesy of 2004, Mr. President, I was inspired in 2005 by the spirit to do a *CD*—a tribute to Ray Charles in social humor. Entitled: From Beyond-The Genius Goes On: I Can't See Shit! The premise was that while in trance, I became a medium for the spirit of Ray Charles, who speaks on a variety of subjects.

For example, 9/11, a conspiracy. *Founding Fathers. The Carpet Baggers of Wall Street. Bush-Wackers,* etc. Ray gives notification of a real bright light—Mr. Barack Obama. The light of—the audacity to hope—*change has come! This is audacious!*

As time passed and time passes quickly! Time is a lot like gas, sometimes it passes unnoticed, and then there it is! Two thousand and six—***BAM!*** In yo' face as Mr. Obama declares his intention to run for the **big seat.** A black face in the race. Suddenly, in a blink of an eye, it's February som'em two thousand and eight as I stand eyeball to eyeball with Mr. Roy Rogers. *Oden Kamp.*

We're scantily dressed. Okay, if it weren't for the towels wrapped around our midsection, we were butt naked, all right! You got me. I'm back at the YMCA. You know it builds strong bodies, families, and communities! Okay! *SNAP, SNAP!*

Anyway, Roy has this look, you know, that look when someone has already volunteered you for something, and now they must con you into volunteering yourself. Roy took a coy, cordial approach. Diplomatic and especially charming. He approaches me with, "Mick E., how do you feel about Barack Obama?"

I smiled like a man who had been shot with a loaded question, and as if mortally wounded, I responded, "How do you want me to feel?" There was a silent gasp. Roy interpreted that as a **YES!** and began dictating the rules of engagement.

"Mick E., you should write a piece on Obama. You should . . . why?" He didn't give me a chance to respond, as he rolled right along telling me why. "I'll tell you why! One, you have a way of saying things. Secondly, you'll say something unique and befitting to Mr. Obama."

Needless to say, I took the assignment. Fulfilling the prophecy. Mr. Barack Obama, *the vision of change.* Because where there is no vision, people perish. And where there is vision, prophecy precedes. So moving forward, I preceded to write *Dear Mr. President:* It was a filmed presentation airing on YouTube, February 22, 2008. The prophecy fulfilled. It is written. You can google this up under Mick E. Jones, you'll be surprised what else pops up!

November 4 and the fulfillment! Mr. Barack Obama, the president of the United States and the prime minister of peace and goodwill to the world. ***In God We Trust,*** not politics! This is **the change** . . . *read the money!*

Finally, my brother, Mr. President. Again, congratulations. Now! Really get your act together.

> *Be strong in the Lord and in the power of His might. Put on the whole armor of God, that you may be able to stand against the wiles of the devil. For we do not wrestle against flesh and blood, but against principalities, against powers, against the rulers of the darkness of this age, against spiritual hosts of wickedness in the heavenly places.*
>
> Ephesians 6:10-12

A tribute to Mr. Albert Crane my friend and brother—who is, deceased. Rest in peace my dear friend and so cherished brother in Christ.

TRUTH LIES IN WAIT

What is politically correct
may be morally expedient,
but is spiritually bankrupt!

—Albert Crane

The ramifications of these widely used social elements creates an interesting dilemma in relationships, namely, computer-generated data streams fabricating an unsubstantiated truth based entirely upon the veracity of biased information. It's the ability to create one thing from another and call it fact. The use of this product has led to a culture where **primary truth** is a second-rate commodity.

It comes when we create from what is known a new and more pleasing ideology, thereby nurturing a culture, which feels comfortable with what we call **plastic truth. Primary truth**, when cleverly manipulated, becomes a viable polymer that's molded to fit our personal agenda.

Political correctness is essentially **plastic truth**.

268

Whereas *moral expediency* can be likened to living in the fast lane. Do or say whatever it takes to get the desired results.

Spiritual bankruptcy comes when man supersedes God. It is the inherent fallibility of *political correctness* and *moral expedience.*

To illustrate, some years ago, there was an incident involving a theater patron who yelled, **"FIRE! FIRE!"** Panic erupted, and someone was trampled to death as the theater goers emptied out onto the street in a stampede. As a result, it became *law* that anyone who provoked a riot, created an opportunity for civil unrest or falsely created social panic, is guilty of a crime. Yet it's a crime committed at the highest levels of government by the most respected leaders of our day. Although the theater incident happened years ago, we, like the theater patron, still fabricate panic, give credibility to provocative statements, which are not true, and condone unrest created in the wake of those allegations.

During the past few years, this moral triad has found new advocates when a pilot of an airplane flew into the World Trade Center tower. Somewhere, an air traffic controller noted irregularities in the flight of the aircraft and notified authorities of a potential disaster in the making. No one really believed his story. Minutes later, the plane crashed into tower number 1. Then, a second plane crashed into tower number 2. Now an attitude of fear reigned, fueled by scores of bureaucratically sanctioned overrides, thereby scrambling our ability to mobilize a timely strategic defense. We panicked, and a stampede ensued. The stock market plunged, and the morale of the nation dipped as fear gripped our nation.

As minutes elapsed, people were dying in New York, Washington, and Pennsylvania. In what may be regarded as one of history's most calamitous events, the president, offsetting this monumental failure, rallied the nation around a *politically correct, morally expedient truth:* **Let's get the person responsible!**

That person was named: **Osama bin Laden**—a rogue terrorist born to a wealthy oil family in Arabia and trained by high level U.S. operatives during the early days of the Russian invasion of Afghanistan. His claim that America is Satan in disguise became his call to arms. He became the *poster child* for a *jihadist-style* terrorist network powered by those who, likewise, believed America to be the root of evil. *The jihad's* primary directive is to kill all *infidels* who do not submit to *Allah's* supremacy as it was written by the Prophet Muhammad in the book entitled the *Holy Qur'an* in 725 AD.

Our response was overwhelmingly supportive for finding and bringing this horrible person to justice on the stage of world opinion. He *must* be found, silenced, debriefed, and dehumanized, then dragged out onto the world stage where he could be properly vilified. As a nation, his whereabouts became paramount.

As our effort began to become *morally expedient,* we allocated large sums of money, troops, sleuths, intel co-ops, and any resource suitable to ferret out this foreign heretic and madman. When we were unable to apprehend this mysteriously elusive heathen, we called out an army of *politically correct, morally expedient* assassins to create chaos and unhinge the world's view of itself and launch a unilateral offensive against any person suspected of being involved in this tragic American event.

Unfortunately, this avenue of attack disenfranchised America from the rest of the world, failing to provide us with our objective: ***Osama bin Laden***.

As time passed, America spent more money in search of one man than what we had spent on World War II. In view of the distress we felt in having our sovereignty violated, it became apparent that our military might was required. Therefore, we brought to bear a mighty military machine against an impoverished third world nation far from our shores. We believed Osama bin Laden had been tucked away in a remote cave in the Kyber Pass region separating Afghanistan and Pakistan. The Afghan government of the day were Islamic fundamentalist known as the Taliban. They were found to be oppressing Afghan women and were, summarily, branded zealots. Under the guise of finding the mastermind of the World Trade Center inferno, our president declared the Taliban to be terrorists, thus entitling America to enter into Afghanistan and bring justice to bear. In retrospect, we created chaos, caused death, empowered and enriched criminals overnight, and ultimately, divided the world into two opposing—a *spiritually bankrupt* position for a world now seriously traumatized by the ongoing events of our *politically correct, morally expedient* modality for bringing justice to bear.

Like the theater patron who falsely screamed, **"FIRE! FIRE!"**, our vice president alluded to the president that Iraq and its leader, a notorious tyrant, had developed Weapons of Mass Destruction! This news spread like wildfire, and heads turned.

A cadre of men and women were deployed by those advocating this position. They were armed with supportive evidence detailing *the truth* of this treachery. They were given hall passes to run through the Rooms of Power in Washington, yelling, "They are in Iraq! They are in Afghanistan! They are in the hands of the Islamic terrorists! Look what they have done! See for yourselves!"

During the intervening months, Arab-generated propaganda had transformed **Osama bin Laden** into a legend. **Where in the world is Osama bin Laden?**

Americans, anxious for results, had been stoked with the notion Iraq was deeply involved. Fired by *moral expediency,* we armed ourselves with advanced weapons of war. With our engagement in Afghanistan in full force, we were being stretched to the limit, yet the *triad of deception* continued to grow in strength and urgency.

In eighteen months, America went from a *good neighbor, strong ally,* and *benevolent caregiver* to an aggressive giant circling the planet with an avenging heart. Through unnamed sources, we learned Iraq was apparently in collusion with the hated *bin Laden* and **had** Weapons of Mass Destruction, which was utterly unacceptable. It was generally believed, due in part to the continual media focus on establishing homeland security, that Islamic terrorists would launch an attack as part of their plan to wipe out all *infidels!*

Thus, the birth of the modern *preemptive attack. Politically correct, morally expedient, and spiritually bankrupt,* we bombed Baghdad vicariously over CNN.

Countless bodies lay dead in the streets as squads of highly trained SWAT teams searched the city for the treacherous, sadistic tyrant beholden to *Islamic jihadists,* especially **Osama bin Laden**, who had ordered an attack on America!

Computer-guided *smart bombs* wove their way through city streets, slicing the velvet blue of the Arabian sky, destroying a world capitol in minutes. Undeterred, U.S. missiles crisscrossed the heavens in search of predetermined targets. Simultaneously, we continued our military assault and political dissection of Afghanistan.

Meanwhile, the American public sat glued to their televisions, transfixed by the pyrotechnics provided by our rockets, let alone the breakneck speed at which foot soldiers poured out across the Iraqi desert on their way to *liberate* Baghdad.

America humbled the Iraqi people, defamed their culture, and ultimately opened the door for the desecration of their holiest of institutions and centers of culture. Like the story of the theater patron who yelled, **"FIRE! FIRE!"**, there were no Weapons of Mass Destruction. The evildoer who ordered destruction and fire upon America has never been found. Yet we upended two nations, leveled homes, destroyed holy sites, and killed scores of innocent people. In the eyes of many, we had become *spiritually bankrupt.*

The men and women who had set their sights on this noble endeavor were hard-pressed to escape the devastation created in the aftermath of their wrath. As the dust settled, they looked around the Rooms of Power asking if anyone knew how this came to be. Many opined sadly it was misinterpreted intelligence information, others a case of self-preservation. Many simply surfed the *Internet* looking for more visual footage of the carnage we were delivering so handily.

Truth took a nosedive. We had created a virtual reality, complete with video games, visual aids, statistics, fear-filled options, all the while packaging **primary truth** into nondescript boxes labeled Classified National Security and storing them in some secret location operated by clandestine agencies of the government.

We were directed to idolize our troops and hail our war machines the best in the world. No one would or could stand up to our fearful presence. We told ourselves that whatever it took was the right response! We went to church asking God to watch over us and give us victory. Were we victorious?

In an updated analysis, we are politically isolated, morally bankrupt, and spiritually devastated. ***Truth lies in wait*** until that day when we publicly acknowledge our sins and seek forgiveness. We have delivered a savage blow to the planet in the name of the game of **Gotcha!** And what did we get? Zilch, zero, nada, nothing but trouble, and a multitrillion-dollar deficit fueled largely by our dependence on *materialism, militarism, and mania.* We stand to face a judgment that will be anything but lenient.

Perhaps there should be a law against such folly.

THE END

CPSIA information can be obtained
at www.ICGtesting.com
Printed in the USA
FFHW020033280119
50302702-55373FF